MANAGING THE MANAGER

WHY IT FEELS LIKE YOU DON'T HAVE HELP

"REDEFINING CHANGE LEADERSHIP IN THE TECHNOLOGICAL AGE"

MICHAEL C TOBIAS

Copyright © 2024 Michael C. Tobias

All Rights Reserved

Table of Contents

Introduction: Navigating Myths And Realities In The Technological Leadership Landscape *1*

Chapter 1: Redefining Change Leadership In The Technological Age *3*

    Managers Still Do Not Listen Though 7

    The Changing Landscape of Managerial Expertise — A CEO's Perspective on Navigating Generational and Technological Shifts .12

Chapter 2: The False Narrative of Change Resistance *31*

    Understanding The "Permafrost" Layer 31

    The Myth Of Resistant Middle Managers 31

Chapter 3: The Role Of Target Outcomes *45*

    The Importance Of Clear Outcomes 45

    Financial Targets And Fundamental Change 46

    Activities vs. Outcomes: Bridging the Gap 46

Chapter 4: Maximizing Leadership Potential In The Digital Age *78*

    Investing In Personal And Organizational Resilience 79

    The Program Emphasized Several Core Principles 81

Chapter 5: The Interplay Between Leadership And Middle Management *85*

    Taming The Fire: A CEO's Guide To Managing The Angry Manager 87

    The Diplomacy Dilemma: Managing The Overly Nice Manager — A CEO's Viewpoint 93

    Navigating The Labyrinth Of Leadership And Middle Management Dynamics 98

Chapter 6: Beyond Monetary Motivations: Providing Clarity And Direction *108*

    The Myth Of Monetary Motivation 108

The Necessity Of Hands-On Leadership: Steering The Ship With Foresight 116

Albert" BEYOND Monetary Motivations: Providing Clarity and Direction 120

Chapter 7: Cultivating A Thriving Managerial Ecosystem: Deepening The Roots Of Leadership 122

Deepening The Roots Of Leadership: Seizing Every Opportunity 124

Leading By Example: An Unwavering Commitment To Excellence 127

Chapter 8: The Legacy Of Leadership: Crafting A Managerial Blueprint For The Future 136

Foresight In Technological Evolution 136

The Ripple Effect Of Managerial Decisions 138

Part 2: The Inner Ladder: Weighing The Pros And Cons Of Promoting From Within A CEO's Perspective 142

Redefining Managerial Training: A Paradigm Shift For The 21st Century Workforce 159

The Cox Methodology: A Beacon for Modern Management 202

The Turnaround: Leading Through Crisis in the COVID Era 219

Final Words: The Chain Reaction of Purposeful Leadership 224

INTRODUCTION: NAVIGATING MYTHS AND REALITIES IN THE TECHNOLOGICAL LEADERSHIP LANDSCAPE

In a world where algorithms predict our next purchase and virtual meetings dominate our calendars, the essence of work has witnessed a tectonic shift. With this technological evolution, there has been a simultaneous transformation in our understanding of leadership and management. But have we truly grasped the nuanced changes, or are we being led astray by age-old myths and outdated narratives?

The picture painted of the modern manager is often unflattering. Labeled as "lazy" or "resistant to change," they are depicted as obstacles in the path of visionary leaders trying to usher in a new era. But as with many myths, there's more than meets the eye. Is it possible that in our haste to champion the age of technology, we've misplaced our blame, neglecting to see the real heroes and true challenges?

In "Managing the Manager," we embark on a journey to dissect these misconceptions to understand the very fabric of work ethics in this new world. We delve into the layers of organizational change, dispelling the notion of the resistant middle manager and highlighting the overlooked role of outcomes in driving success. We will explore how to create certain obligations and accountability benchmarks for your staff.

As we turn our gaze towards leadership, a surprising revelation awaits. Could it be that our leaders, with their lofty visions, are the ones falling short? Through meticulous research and eye-opening narratives, we shed light on the actual impediments to change and the unsung heroics of our managers. Maybe we are right, though, as Managers just do not support the company unless they are supported in turn.

Beyond just identification, this book serves as a guide, paving the way for companies to adapt and thrive. With actionable insights on leadership training, the value of continuous feedback, and the indispensability of understanding our new technological playground, we present a roadmap to a future where managers are empowered, leaders are proactive, and organizations are poised for success. You will find short stories to use as examples and perspectives from a CEO of a large sales company. The information you will read is from the real world and carefully laid out to speak in reality about what can be done and how we are all alike.

So, as we stand on the precipice of this exploration, we invite you to challenge your beliefs, look beyond the myths, and embrace a new understanding of leadership in the technological age. Welcome to a journey of discovery, reflection, and transformation. Within the bustling dynamics of our offices, I've always instilled an ethos that ensures we remain at the forefront of change and leadership challenges. This isn't just about keeping pace; it's about setting the pace. I firmly believe that complacency is the first step towards obsolescence. Thus, I embed in our organizational culture the practice of 'never-ending improvement.' It's not merely a catchphrase but a lived reality for us. By constantly reflecting, refining, and reinventing, we not only address current challenges but preemptively prepare for future ones. This proactive stance ensures our team doesn't just react to change but actively shapes it, positioning us as leaders in our domain.

Chapter 1: Redefining Change Leadership In The Technological Age

In the bustling corridors of corporate offices, coffee shops, and virtual meeting rooms, a recurring narrative has been playing out for decades. It's a story that paints a picture of dynamic leaders battling stagnation, trying to infuse change and innovation into their organizations, only to be held back by middle managers – the supposed 'permafrost' layer that resists transformation. Such managers, long-serving and experienced, are often depicted as hesitant, if not obstructive, to the grand visions of their upper management.

But as the digital age unfolds, enveloping industries with its vast technological advances, from AI-driven insights to the sheer speed of information dissemination, the truth behind this narrative is under the microscope. How can managers, central to the translation of strategies into tangible actions, be the only roadblocks? Are our organizations suffering from a flawed narrative?

Take "Kodak", for instance. A titan in its time, it failed to capitalize on its digital camera invention due to a lack of strategic foresight by its top leadership, not because middle managers refused to adapt. On the other hand, we have "Netflix," which transitioned from a mail-order DVD service to a streaming behemoth. This wasn't just because of a visionary leader but also due to a managerial force that could pivot, adapt, and implement change effectively.

Or consider "Nokia," a name synonymous with mobile phones in the early 2000s. Their decline was not solely a result of middle management resistance but more from a leadership blindspot in recognizing the shift to smartphones and their potential impact. In contrast, "Microsoft," under Satya Nadella's leadership, metamorphosed from a company once fixated on Windows to embracing cloud computing, open-source platforms, and more. But Nadella wasn't working in isolation. He empowered managers and teams to bring about this change, reshaping the company's destiny.

Our world, particularly the business landscape, is under a state of constant flux, made even more pronounced by technological advancements. In such a scenario, blaming a singular layer of an organization's hierarchy for failed change initiatives is not just simplistic but potentially detrimental. As we embark on this journey to redefine change leadership in our digital age, we will debunk myths, lean into research, and aim to understand where the true essence of change management lies – and how best to harness it.

Hold on tight. The narrative you once believed is about to be reshaped...

Redefining Change Leadership in the Technological Age

The role of the manager has undergone significant evolution over the past few years, largely influenced by external factors such as technological advancements, societal expectations, and global disruptions like the pandemic. Traditionally, managers were the helm of operational processes - their primary role was to evaluate and oversee the performance of employees within a set framework. But as we edge deeper into the technological age, it becomes imperative to redefine what change leadership truly entails.

Let's take a look at three pivotal trends that are driving this shift:

The Normalization of Remote Work

Remote work has become the new normal, reshaping the dynamics of employee-manager relationships. With over 70% of these relationships operating in a partially remote environment, the synchronous nature of work is giving way to more asynchronous engagements. Managers no longer have the immediate oversight they once had. This shift necessitates a change in focus - from closely monitoring processes to emphasizing outputs. The day-to-day visibility into an employee's work routine diminishes, placing outcomes at the center of performance evaluations. The shift to remote work has become a hallmark of the modern business era, with many hailing it as the 'new normal.' While there are undeniable advantages, including flexibility and work-life balance, we've noticed a concerning trend within our company. After the initial one to three months of transitioning to work-from-home setups, there's been a palpable dip in production among our sales teams. It appears that the home environment, despite its comforts, may not be as stimulating or motivating as the collaborative and competitive atmosphere of the office. The absence of immediate team dynamics, spontaneous brainstorming sessions, and the palpable energy of a buzzing sales floor seems to gradually erode the drive that fuels our sales force.

Boosting remote motivation requires a mix of tailored strategies, technological tools, and a genuine understanding of individual needs.

Here are some effective approaches to elevate motivation in a remote setup:

Managers should maintain regular one-on-one check-ins with team members. These sessions serve as a platform for employees to discuss challenges, provide updates, and feel connected to the organization's pulse. Clearly defined goals provide direction and purpose. When employees understand what's expected and the impact of their roles, they are more motivated to deliver. Organize virtual team-building events and activities. This can range from professional workshops to casual game nights. Such events help in fostering camaraderie among remote workers. Publicly acknowledge and reward employees for their achievements. Recognition can be a powerful motivator. Tools like 'Employee of the Month' awards, virtual shout-outs, or even bonus structures for significant achievements can boost morale. Ensure your team has access to efficient collaboration tools. Platforms like Slack, Microsoft Teams, or Zoom can simulate the office environment to some extent and keep communication channels open.

Offer opportunities for professional development. Webinars, online courses, or workshops can give employees a sense of growth and a break from the usual routine. Understand that working from home can come with its set of distractions. Offering flexibility in work hours can help employees manage their time better and enhance productivity. Implement platforms or channels where employees can voice their concerns or suggestions. Feeling heard can enhance motivation. Working remotely can sometimes lead to feelings of isolation or burnout. Provide resources, talks, or counseling services that address mental well-being. Tools like Sococo or Tandem can simulate an office environment where employees can 'walk' over to a colleague's desk, enhancing the feeling of connectedness.

6

Physical well-being is often linked to mental motivation. Encourage regular breaks, and perhaps even offer virtual workout sessions or challenges to keep the team active. Remind your team of the company's mission and vision and how their role, even if remote, plays a crucial part in the bigger picture. By implementing these strategies and maintaining a genuine dialogue with your remote employees, you can foster an environment of motivation and productivity, bridging the gap posed by physical distances.

Evolving Employee Expectations

The pandemic, while disruptive, has also ushered in an era of enhanced organizational support in areas such as mental health and childcare. Consequently, the boundary between professional and personal spheres is blurring. Employees now view managers not just as supervisors but as vital components of their holistic support system. The expectation is clear: managers should enhance not only the employee experience but also their broader life experience.

MANAGERS STILL DO NOT LISTEN THOUGH

Reimagining Leadership and Management: Bridging the Gap Between Vision and Execution — A CEO's Perspective

In today's intricate and rapidly evolving landscape, the traditional paradigms of management are undergoing a significant transformation. Although foundational management skills like goal-setting, planning, employee motivation, and coaching remain invaluable, these practices alone are insufficient for navigating the complexities of modern organizational life.

Our hyperconnected, technology-driven world demands more from those who are not just managing processes but leading transformative change.

So, what does leadership mean in this nuanced context? Leadership transcends managerial competencies to become an orchestration of vision, inspiration, and actionable change. A leader doesn't just set the course but engages everyone in moving toward it. Leaders see the bigger picture; they recognize the opportunities embedded in the disruptive forces that may be unsettling their industries. They are visionaries who energize their organizations to transform challenges into avenues for growth.

Leadership in this context goes beyond skill and enters the realm of character. Integrity and credibility are not just buzzwords; they are the bedrock upon which trust is built. Trust is the currency of any change initiative. When people trust their leaders, they are more willing to venture into the unknown and take the risks that come with any transformational effort.

It's not just about setting a vision; it's about equipping your managers with the ability to enact it. This means a paradigm shift is in order — managers can no longer afford to be mere operators; they must also be innovators and catalysts for change. They need to understand the intricacies of their industry's latest trends, technologies, and customer behaviors. They must be able to pivot, adapt, and lead their teams into new territories, even when the map is unclear.

To move beyond conventional management activities, managers must be trained to think like change leaders. This involves programs focused not just on skills but also on mindset and vision. Scenario planning, strategic foresight, and resilience training should be as commonplace as performance reviews and budget planning.

To operationalize this leadership vision, there must be alignment between the activities of management and the overarching goals of leadership. This involves breaking down silos that exist between different layers and departments in the organization. Every initiative, project, and task should clearly connect back to the larger vision. If your management team cannot draw a line from what they do daily to where the company is headed, then there's a disconnect that needs addressing.

Finally, in an age where change is the only constant, fostering a culture of continuous learning and adaptability is key. Organizations that can collectively learn and adapt are the ones that will not just survive but thrive. Managers, who are now change leaders, should be at the forefront of fostering this culture. They should be role models of adaptability, continuous learning, and resilience.

The days of managers merely keeping the ship steady are long gone. In today's volatile business environment, they must also be the navigators, the visionaries, and the change-makers. As a CEO, my role is not just to lead but to empower my managers to become the kind of leaders who can guide the organization toward a future that may be uncertain but is ripe with opportunities for those willing and able to seize them.

Even as CEO, I make it a point to personally lead sales meetings and training sessions for both our salespeople and the management team. I believe that staying hands-on in these critical areas sends a powerful message: we're all in this together, and we all have roles to play in understanding and driving our business forward. Conducting these meetings allows me to share my insights and strategies for staying ahead of the curve, but it also provides a forum for real-time feedback and discussion. The collaborative setting reinforces that no one is above the work, and we all need to fully grasp our business from the ground up to be effective. It's this collective understanding and shared effort that positions us to outperform the competition and achieve our ambitious goals.

A key facet of accountable leadership extends beyond mere conduct to encapsulate an ingrained attitude of responsibility. This attitude is not only evident in visible actions but also manifests subtly in various nuanced behaviors. Importantly, in my workplace, this responsibility is a shared trait, exhibited not just by the leader but also by all the managers who diligently account for their respective job duties.

The essence of this leadership begins with a deeply felt, almost instinctive, connection to the organization. Leaders and managers alike experience genuine pride when the organization thrives and feels a sense of discomfort during its challenging phases. This emotional investment creates an indomitable bond. There is an unambiguous understanding that personal ambitions are secondary to the collective objectives, which, in turn, always yield to the overarching needs of the organization.

Accountable leadership also encompasses actions that may not offer immediate rewards but contribute to the organization's long-term wellbeing. For instance, nurturing future leaders is often an unrewarded endeavor. There may be no immediate incentives for executives who invest time and effort into the growth and development of emerging leaders. Nonetheless, in my organization, leaders and managers continue to prioritize this critical function, understanding its intrinsic value, even if it doesn't result in immediate recognition or tangible rewards. In my role as the CEO of a sales company, I frequently encounter managers who bemoan their perceived lack of authority. What they often miss is that authority is a byproduct of demonstrated responsibility. It's not something handed down from above but earned through consistent, responsible behavior. Peter Drucker aptly noted, "Management has no power. Management has only responsibility." I wholeheartedly agree with this sentiment. For leaders to wield meaningful influence, they must not only embody responsible behavior but also demand it from their team members.

So, how can one bolster their sense of responsibility? The initial step is a paradigm shift in thinking. As a leader, you are not solely accountable for your individual results but for the collective performance of your team. The measure of your success transitions from your personal accomplishments to the achievements of your entire organization. This can be a difficult adjustment, and some unfortunately never make the leap, often to their own and their team's detriment.

The next step is embracing what I call the "responsibility-authority paradox." When your responsible conduct aligns with your attitude of responsibility, you unlock a potent form of influence that can fast track your growth as a leader. In the sales world, this is not just about hitting quotas or closing deals; it's about creating a culture of accountability, where everyone from managers to sales representatives is vested in the overarching goals of the organization. Through this dual approach, you're not just leading; you're empowering others to lead, thereby creating a cycle of shared success and leadership growth.

The Changing Landscape of Managerial Expertise — A CEO's Perspective on Navigating Generational and Technological Shifts

The Obsolescence of Experience

In my earlier years as a manager, I, like many of my peers, took great pride in my experience. It was the yardstick by which we measured our competence, our authority, and our value to the organization. But times have changed drastically. We're at an inflection point where experience, once the gold standard of managerial acumen, is becoming less of a universally acknowledged asset. The generational gap between my managerial style and that of the younger crop—primarily those 35 or under—is not just a subtle shift but a seismic one.

Young managers today prioritize knowledge and learning agility over experience. They have a knack for synthesizing information quickly, extracting insights, and putting them into action—something that took many of us older managers years, if not decades, to do effectively. For those of us who have invested our entire careers in amassing experience, this shift can be disconcerting. The younger generation expects us to adapt, to model the kind of knowledge-based decision-making that they are already comfortable with. And this leads to a conundrum—how do we merge these two divergent philosophies in a managerial approach?

The Need for Young Leadership

Herein lies a critical takeaway for any forward-looking organization: the need to elevate younger individuals to significant roles sooner than we might have considered prudent in the past. This isn't just a nod to generational equity but a strategic imperative. The speed of technological change and the freshness of perspective that younger minds bring are assets that businesses can't afford to ignore.

The old practice of replacing a 65-year-old executive with a 59-year-old one needs reevaluation. It's time to look toward the savvy 35-year-olds who speak the language of today's digital economy. Their value isn't measured by years of experience but by their ability to understand and leverage current technologies, adapt to rapid changes, and bring a fresh perspective to old problems.

Technology as the New Frontier

It would be unwise to downplay the role of technology in this paradigm shift. While traditional sectors like automotive or steel still have relevance, they are no longer the torchbearers of innovation they once were. Future economic growth is more likely to be driven by industries rooted in emerging technologies. Whether it's renewable energy, AI, or biotechnology, the new engines of economic growth are clearly mapped out for those willing to see them.

Many established sectors find themselves on the defensive, having to adapt to technological advancements that could potentially upend their markets. The automobile industry, for instance, must grapple with the looming reality of electric vehicles and potential bans on fossil-fuel-powered cars in urban areas. Likewise, industries like steel, while still relevant, must evolve significantly to regain their former stature, facing competition from alternative materials and new manufacturing techniques.

In my business, as our agency evolves, we're making a strategic shift towards becoming a tech company, with a particular focus on developing artificial intelligence solutions in our centers. This transformation is driven by the recognition that technology is revolutionizing our industry, and to stay competitive, we must be at the forefront of innovation. We are investing in R&D, collaborating with experts in the field, and upskilling our team to meet the challenges and opportunities that AI presents. Our aim is to not only integrate these advanced technologies into our own operations but also to commercialize them, offering cutting-edge solutions to clients and the broader market. By actively steering our agency in this direction, we are positioning ourselves for long-term success and industry leadership in an increasingly tech-driven world.

Convergence and Adaptation: The Way Forward

As a CEO navigating this transformative landscape, my role becomes that of a bridge builder, connecting the wisdom accumulated from years of experience with the innovative approaches brought by younger generations. Organizations must create environments where these different forms of expertise not only co-exist but complement each other.

We must also recognize that the very metrics by which we measure success and managerial effectiveness are evolving. While experience will never be completely obsolete—it still offers invaluable insights into human behavior, relationships, and instinctual decision-making—its monopoly as the primary asset for leadership is over.

The mandate for contemporary businesses is clear: embrace the transition from an experience-first to a knowledge-first managerial approach, integrate younger leaders more quickly into significant roles, and adapt to technological realities that are changing the very fabric of various industries. It's not just about staying current; it's about staying ahead. Failure to adapt is not an option if the goal is sustainable growth and relevance in this ever-changing business landscape.

The New Metrics of Accountability

Another key aspect of this transformation is how we measure managerial effectiveness and hold managers accountable. Gone are the days when a manager's performance could be evaluated purely on short-term output or financial metrics. Today's complex and fast-paced business environment demands a more nuanced approach to managerial performance reviews.

Now more than ever, managers must be held accountable for softer metrics such as employee engagement, team cohesion, adaptability to change, and the ability to foster a culture of continuous learning and innovation. This requires a new kind of performance review—ongoing, multidimensional, and aligned with the values and objectives of the organization.

As a CEO, I recognize the importance of setting the tone for this change. Executive leadership needs to actively engage with managers, providing continuous feedback and development opportunities rather than confining evaluations to annual reviews. We also must leverage technology to gain real-time insights into performance, utilizing data analytics to offer a more comprehensive and timely understanding of both individual and team effectiveness.

I also understand that different generations have unique expectations, communication styles, and working habits. In particular, the rise of remote work and digital transformation has significant implications for managing Gen Z employees. This younger workforce has grown up in a digital-first environment and values flexibility, autonomy, and digital literacy. For older generations of managers accustomed to in-person supervision and traditional 9-to-5 workdays, adapting to this new reality can be challenging. But adapt we must.

Younger managers may naturally be more attuned to this digital ecosystem, but they also benefit from the emotional intelligence and people management skills that come with experience. Therefore, creating mentorship programs where younger managers can learn from more experienced ones, and vice versa, can foster a more collaborative and productive work environment.

The COVID-19 pandemic and the subsequent rise of remote work have accelerated changes that were already in motion. Managers now need skills in managing remote teams, something that was not a core competency for many of us until recently. Building team cohesion, maintaining productivity, and ensuring mental well-being have all become challenges in a remote setting. These skills need to be integrated into managerial training programs urgently, with a keen focus on results rather than time spent in a physical office.

The underpinning theme here is simple: change is not just imminent; it is already here. As business leaders, we can either embrace it or face the risk of becoming obsolete. Integrating younger talent, re-evaluating performance metrics, leveraging technology, and adapting to new ways of work are not just trendy talking points; they are necessities.

Our businesses are not isolated islands but evolving ecosystems. As I see it, my role as a CEO is to ensure that this ecosystem remains balanced yet agile, rooted in foundational principles, yet open to change, valuing experience, yet hungry for innovation. Only by accomplishing this delicate balance can we hope to navigate the complex and ever-changing waters of today's business environment successfully.

Evolving Employee Expectations: Navigating New Norms in Hybrid Work At My Company

In the labyrinth of modern corporate structures, change is the only constant. And nowhere has this been more evident than in the dramatic shifts we've witnessed in the post-pandemic era. As the world grappled with unforeseen challenges, our company, too, found itself at the nexus of evolving employee expectations and the imperative of business continuity.

The pandemic's onslaught didn't just change the way we worked; it transformed how we perceived work and its place in our lives. Physical offices, once buzzing hubs of collaboration, became eerily quiet as homes turned into makeshift workspaces. The lines between professional responsibilities and personal commitments became blurred, setting in motion a profound transformation in workplace dynamics.

Gone are the days when employees viewed their jobs as mere sources of income. In today's world, they seek a holistic experience, one where their employers understand, acknowledge, and cater to their multifaceted needs. This transformation isn't just about flexible work hours or the provision of ergonomic furniture for home offices. It delves deeper, touching the very core of human needs: mental well-being and emotional support.

Recognizing this, our company has taken strides to ensure that our employees, whether they're working from the office or their living rooms, feel supported and understood. Mental health, once a taboo topic in corporate corridors, has come to the forefront. We've initiated programs that allow employees to discuss their anxieties, stresses, and challenges openly. By partnering with counseling services and hosting regular well-being webinars, we're signaling a clear message: we care about your mental well-being as much as we do about your professional output.

Childcare, another critical aspect, has also witnessed a reimagining. Understanding that working parents might struggle with managing their professional commitments while ensuring their children's well-being, we've initiated support groups and flexible work arrangements. This approach allows parents to balance their roles without feeling overwhelmed.

As the boundary between personal and professional realms becomes porous, the role of managers in our organization has seen a metamorphosis. No longer are they just taskmasters or project overseers. Instead, they've evolved into mentors, guides, and, in many cases, confidantes.

Employees now look up to their managers not just for professional guidance but also for personal support. This shift has necessitated training programs that equip our managers with skills beyond the conventional. Emotional intelligence, empathy, and active listening have become as crucial as strategy formulation or project management.

Navigating these evolving expectations hasn't been a walk in the park. It has required introspection, adaptability, and, above all, a genuine commitment to our employees' holistic well-being. But as we forge ahead, we do so with the confidence that these changes, though challenging, are steering us towards a more inclusive, empathetic, and human-centric corporate landscape.

In embracing these shifts, our company isn't just fulfilling immediate needs; we're crafting a legacy—a legacy of understanding, support, and genuine care. And as we've come to realize, in the world of modern business, this might just be our most invaluable asset.

Technological Augmentation in Employee Management

The accelerated adoption of technology, especially during the pandemic, is rewriting managerial functions. Companies are not just leveraging technology to streamline employee tasks but are also integrating it to automate traditional managerial roles. With tools ranging from AI-driven feedback systems to sophisticated scheduling software, the very essence of management is undergoing transformation. Forecasts suggest that by 2024, technology could potentially replace up to 69% of tasks traditionally performed by managers.

These trends point towards a broader change: the pivot from "seeing" to "feeling." In this new era, the emphasis is less on observing what employees are doing and more on understanding how they feel. A manager's role transitions from being a mere supervisor to a mentor, guide, and emotional anchor.

The technological age demands a fresh perspective on change leadership. Managers, in this new paradigm, are not just taskmasters but empathetic leaders attuned to the emotional and professional needs of their teams. Embracing this change is not just necessary; it's vital for the evolution and success of organizations in the modern world.

The Evolution of Supervision

The modern business ecosystem, marred by unpredictable challenges and fueled by rapid technological advancements, is seeing a profound change in managerial roles. Central to this transformation is the union of technology with management functions, a trend that took root, especially during the recent global crisis.

At the heart of our organization's pioneering approach to employee management lies our suite of in-house software programs fortified by Artificial Intelligence. These tools are not just ancillary aids but pivotal pillars in our management strategy. With these advanced systems, we can meticulously track production metrics, gain insights from call audits, and dynamically manage workloads.

Yet, while these technological marvels equip us with unparalleled oversight, they also point towards a profound philosophical shift. In the past, the primary function of these tools might have been surveillance. Now, however, they are beacons of understanding.

Management, traditionally, was about supervision—ensuring that tasks were completed, standards were met, and deadlines were honored. But, as forecasts suggest, by 2024, a staggering 69% of these routine managerial tasks could be automated. So, where does that leave human managers?

It brings about the monumental pivot from "seeing" to "feeling." With granular task monitoring delegated to software, managers are now free to dive deeper, to understand not just what employees are doing but how they feel while doing it. No longer bound by routine supervisory roles, managers in our organization transform into mentors, guides, and emotional pillars. They become the human touchpoint in a world increasingly governed by code.

While AI and advanced algorithms offer precision, efficiency, and scale, they lack the human facets of empathy, understanding, and compassion. This is where the modern manager steps in, armed with insights gleaned from technology but driven by genuine human connection.

Our managers, aided by our proprietary software, are equipped to address both the tangible and intangible facets of employee experience. They can pinpoint productivity challenges and offer solutions, but they can also sense emotional undercurrents, providing support when needed.

For organizations to flourish in this era, embracing this dual approach is not just advantageous—it's essential. As we sail into the future, we recognize that while technology can inform us, it is the human touch that transforms us. Our organization's marriage of technology with empathetic leadership doesn't just set us up for operational success; it anchors us in values, empathy, and genuine care—a beacon for the future of modern management.

Taking on responsibility is an indispensable element of impactful leadership, a concept thoroughly embodied by my manager, Max, at our healthcare company. Research indicates that teams with responsible individuals create an atmosphere of collaboration, boosting morale and productivity, especially during challenging times. Max is a living testament to this, consistently going above and beyond in his role to the point where he outshines others around him.

At the heart of assuming responsibility is a proactive willingness to confront challenges head-on without waiting for an invitation to do so. This proactive stance could involve assuming new tasks to free up colleagues or identifying and solving problems proactively. When Max takes on these additional responsibilities, he's not just easing his own workload; he's enabling the rest of the team to operate more effectively. He's not the type to point fingers or sit idly by, waiting for circumstances to improve. Instead, he takes the initiative to implement solutions, showcasing an accountability that extends beyond his personal duties to include the well-being of the entire team.

What sets Max apart is not just his sense of responsibility but also his emotional investment in our organization. He feels the highs and lows intensely and gets genuinely emotional when things go awry, clearly reflecting his deep love and commitment to the company. This emotional engagement isn't a sign of weakness; it's a manifestation of his investment in our collective success. Max's approach strengthens not just his own performance but elevates that of individual team members and the team as a whole.

In the complex world of healthcare, where rapid responses and effective team coordination can have life-altering consequences, Max's commitment to responsibility becomes even more invaluable. His willingness to take on more to assume greater responsibilities doesn't just make him an extraordinary leader; it makes our healthcare services more robust, more responsive, and more compassionate. His actions serve as a beacon, inspiring each of us to strive for excellence while nurturing a culture of responsibility and accountability within the organization.

Management, Motivation, and the Role of Technology

The age of automation and artificial intelligence (AI) has dawned upon us, heralding in transformative changes to the workplace. These changes are multifaceted, offering opportunities and challenges in equal measure. At the heart of the discourse around AI's impact is the narrative of human-machine collaboration. Instead of viewing AI as an existential threat to the workforce, a more nuanced perspective suggests that technology, when wielded appropriately, can amplify human capabilities and lead to a harmonious synergy.

The popular narrative paints a picture of AI-driven machines poised to replace humans in various roles. However, a more optimistic and perhaps realistic viewpoint suggests that technology, rather than eliminating jobs, will complement the tasks that humans perform. Instead of a monolithic takeover, we are likely to witness a scenario where technology amplifies human capabilities, augments our creativity, and assists in tasks where computational efficiency is paramount.

Omri Dekalo, CEO of Ubeya, provides valuable insights into the transformative role of technology in the workplace. Contrary to the common misconception that technology would impersonalize and fragment the employer-employee relationship, Dekalo observes the opposite. Technology, especially when chosen and implemented judiciously, can enhance employee engagement, boost satisfaction levels, and bolster productivity.

This resonates with the idea that technology, instead of alienating workers, can be a tool of empowerment. Modern tools can provide real-time feedback, offer flexible work arrangements, enable virtual collaborations, and even customize training modules tailored to individual learning paces. All of these contribute to an enriched employee experience.

The debate on technology and its implications on the workforce is complex. Simplifying it to a binary of "good" or "bad" does a disservice to the multi-dimensional impact technology has on workplaces. This sentiment is echoed by a recent study from the Georgia Institute of Technology and Georgia State University. Their research delves into the lives of those embedded in tech-centric workplaces, offering insights into both the challenges and advantages of such environments.

Working in tech-heavy environments might offer unparalleled access to state-of-the-art tools, real-time data analytics, and seamless collaboration platforms. Yet, it also poses challenges like the constant need to upskill, the pressure to stay updated with rapid technological advancements, and potential issues related to digital well-being.

Management in the digital era must strike a delicate balance. On one hand, there's the allure of efficiency, precision, and scale that technology offers. On the other hand, there's the undeniable human element — the need for empathy, understanding, and personal connection. Leaders must ensure that while they leverage technology to its fullest potential, they do not lose sight of the human values that form the bedrock of any organization.

In the ever-evolving landscape of work, the role of technology is undeniable. However, its impact — positive or negative — is largely contingent on how it's implemented and integrated into the workforce. With thoughtful management strategies and a clear understanding of the nuances of tech-driven workplaces, organizations can harness technology as a force for good, amplifying human potential and fostering a motivated, engaged, and productive workforce.

"In my role as CEO, managing managers is more than just an extension of my strategic responsibilities. It's also about creating an ecosystem where these individuals can both excel in their specific roles and become effective leaders for their teams. Assessing a manager's individual performance might be relatively straightforward—measured in metrics, deliverables, or quarterly objectives. However, gauging their ability to inspire, mentor, and effectively lead a team requires a different toolkit.

Training and development shouldn't be viewed as mere onboarding necessities but as ongoing imperatives. A well-rounded manager needs continuous education in leadership, conflict resolution, and emotional intelligence. Providing such learning opportunities not only equips your managers with the tools they need but also signals the company's investment in their long-term growth.

Regular one-on-one coaching sessions are also invaluable. Far from being a routine performance check, these sessions offer a candid space for managers to discuss challenges, celebrate achievements, and set new benchmarks. They can be invaluable for obtaining insights into the dynamics within teams and the overall effectiveness of a manager's leadership style.

Equally important is the idea of serving as a role model. The axiom 'Do as I say, not as I do' simply has no place in effective leadership. Leadership isn't about perfection; it's about integrity, ownership of one's actions, and setting the behavioral and ethical standards you expect from your managers.

So, in the endeavor to manage managers, remember you're doing more than just overseeing performance—you're shaping the future leaders of your organization."

"Additionally, understanding that each manager has a unique leadership style is crucial. It's not about creating a cadre of managers who all lead in the same way; rather, it's about honing their individual strengths while ensuring a level of consistency in management quality across the board. This nuanced approach allows for a diverse set of leadership styles that can cater to a broad spectrum of employee needs, making for a more inclusive and effective work environment.

Communication is another cornerstone. Open lines of dialogue between you and your managers will pave the way for a healthier organization. This goes beyond just formal reviews or scheduled meetings. Encourage a culture where feedback flows freely in all directions, not just top-down. This mutual exchange of insights will not only enhance transparency but also cultivate a sense of ownership and accountability.

Moreover, remember that technology is your ally. Utilize project management software, feedback tools, and data analytics platforms to gain a clearer picture of how each manager is performing, both as an individual contributor and as a leader.

These tools can offer quantitative backing to the qualitative assessments, giving you a more comprehensive understanding of where each manager excels and where there might be room for improvement.

Lastly, your role in managing managers is not static. The business landscape is ever-changing, influenced by economic fluctuations, technological advancements, and evolving consumer expectations. To navigate these shifts successfully, it's essential to be adaptive and receptive to new management philosophies and techniques. This not only keeps you ahead of the curve but also equips your managers to better handle the complexities and uncertainties of the modern business environment.

The task of managing managers is multi-faceted and ever-evolving. It encompasses everything from fostering professional development and facilitating open communication to setting an example of good leadership and leveraging technology for insights. By attending to these aspects diligently, you are not just overseeing a group of individuals—you are cultivating an elite team of future leaders who will sustain and elevate the organization for years to come." While taking on responsibility unquestionably benefits an organization, it's crucial to acknowledge that leaders can't feasibly shoulder every challenge encountered by their teams. That's why I approach responsibility with a clear intentionality, carefully evaluating where I can most effectively contribute value. Being responsible doesn't mean indiscriminately taking on every task; it means deliberately choosing the responsibilities you know you can fulfill and follow through on.

The act of assuming responsibility needs to be a targeted effort, grounded in the awareness of one's own capabilities and limitations. There are instances where it's not only acceptable but advisable for leaders to decline opportunities that fall outside their skill set or capacity. Although the notion of 'accepting full responsibility' is often championed as a hallmark of exceptional management, the caveat is that this should be done with careful thought to avoid overextension.

My commitment to acting with intention is about striking a balance. It's about assessing each situation and deciding where my involvement would be most beneficial, not just for me but for the entire team. In doing so, I ensure that my actions are not only responsible but also sustainable over the long term. This mindful approach allows me to effectively prioritize tasks, ensuring that I can genuinely commit to and complete the responsibilities I undertake.

By acting with intention, I aim to set a precedent of responsible leadership that is not only ambitious but also realistic. This ethos contributes to building a culture of trust and accountability, where each team member feels supported and empowered to act responsibly within their own roles. In this way, intentional responsibility fosters a healthier, more productive work environment, ultimately benefiting the organization as a whole."

"Albert" Foresight in Technological Evolution

The sun beamed gently through the glass walls of Gorilla Inc's modern office. The spacious workspace, adorned with green plants and ergonomically designed furniture, hummed with the soft clattering of keyboards and occasional friendly banter. It was a seemingly ordinary day, but for Albert, the middle manager of the tech division, the day was anything but ordinary.

Albert had always been a forward-thinker, eager to embrace change and foster innovation. In the ever-evolving world of technology, he believed that complacency was the first step towards obsolescence. That morning, Albert was to present a proposal for integrating a new software platform into the company's workflow - a move he believed would significantly enhance efficiency and offer a competitive edge.

As he made final adjustments to his presentation, Albert anticipated resistance. The existing system had been in place for years and had its advocates. Employees were accustomed to its quirks and had established a comfort zone around it. The challenge for Albert was not just to introduce a new tool but to convey its necessity and long-term benefits.

Standing before the board and his peers, Albert began with a story. He painted a vivid picture of two tech companies from the late 1990s - one that embraced the internet's potential early on and another that hesitated. By the time the latter realized its oversight, it was too late. That company was left in the digital dust while the former soared to unprecedented heights. The message was clear: technological foresight wasn't just about staying current; it was about ensuring survival.

Albert then dove into the specifics of the new software. He showcased its intuitive interface, demonstrated how it could automate redundant tasks, and highlighted the collaborative features that would allow teams to work seamlessly. But more than the features, Albert emphasized the why. He shared data on industry trends, competitors' moves, and projected efficiency gains.

However, the true masterstroke was when Albert presented testimonials from other companies that had adopted the software.

Hearing praises and positive results from peers in the industry made the proposition tangible.

By the end of the presentation, the room was abuzz with excitement. Questions poured in, and while there were concerns, Albert had done his homework. He had anticipated most of the queries and addressed them with data-backed responses.

In the days that followed, Albert took on an even more significant challenge. He organized hands-on workshops, encouraged employees to voice their apprehensions, and provided resources to facilitate the transition. The integration wasn't without its hiccups, but with Albert's proactive approach, the company soon started reaping the benefits of the new system.

Reflection: The inaugural chapter underscores a critical lesson: in the realm of technology, foresight is invaluable. But introducing change is not merely about unveiling a new tool or system; it's about addressing apprehensions, demonstrating value, and ensuring that the team is equipped to embrace the change. Albert's journey in this chapter teaches managers the importance of preparation, persuasion, and persistence in driving technological evolution.

Chapter 2: The False Narrative of Change Resistance

In tales of heroes and villains, it's always easier to have a singular antagonist - a face, an entity, a group that stands in the way of progress. Similarly, in the corporate realm, middle managers have often been painted with a broad brush as the primary culprits resisting change. But is this image accurate? Or is it a scapegoat, conveniently available to explain the pitfalls of unsuccessful transformations?

Understanding The "Permafrost" Layer

Middle managers, often termed the "permafrost," constitute a layer that bridges senior leadership with frontline workers. Their role is both strategic and operational, giving them a unique vantage point. They can see the vision of the leaders and the practicalities and challenges faced by those executing tasks on the ground. Far from being merely resistors, they are often the translators, facilitators, and negotiators of change.

For instance, when "Apple" decided to transition from the traditional iPod to integrating its features into the iPhone, it wasn't just a top-down decision. Middle managers played a crucial role in understanding market demand, aligning teams, and ensuring that the technical challenges were addressed promptly.

The Myth Of Resistant Middle Managers

So, where did this myth originate? One theory is that, as organizational hierarchies formed, senior leaders sought to distance themselves from failures while claiming successes. When a change initiative faltered, middle managers, due to their position and visibility, became an easy target to blame.

However, reality paints a different picture. In "Toyota," the lean manufacturing revolution wasn't just an executive's dream; it involved managers at all levels recognizing inefficiencies, brainstorming solutions, and fostering a culture of continuous improvement.

In another instance, when "IBM" pivoted from being primarily a hardware company to focusing on services and software in the late 20th century, it was the middle managers who read the terrain, communicated the feedback from clients, and drove teams to adapt to new market demands.

Truth Behind the Resistance

Certainly, resistance to change exists. It's a human trait to seek comfort in the familiar. However, branding an entire managerial tier as resistive is an oversimplification.

The Resistance Often Arises From

1. Lack of Clarity: If the vision or strategy isn't clear, managers are left guessing, leading to inaction or wrong actions. In many organizations, it's not uncommon for staff to approach their managers with concerns about not understanding their paychecks. While this could sometimes be a legitimate query due to complex compensation structures or errors, it can also serve as a symptom of a larger issue—employees using lack of understanding as an excuse to avoid accountability or clarity. This may happen because admitting ignorance feels less vulnerable than confronting the possibility of underperformance

or questioning the fairness of the compensation. It's a path of least resistance; saying "I don't understand" is easier and less confrontational than digging deeper into one's own role, responsibilities, or performance metrics that influence compensation. This phenomenon points to a need for greater transparency and education around pay structures, but also for a cultural shift where employees feel comfortable and equipped to engage in more substantive discussions about their roles and contributions.

2. Absence of Resources: Without the necessary tools, personnel, or training, even the most motivated manager can't bring about effective change. In recognizing the need for both convenience and efficiency in today's fast-paced business environment, our company has made a strategic move to centralize all essential resources and tools within our Customer Relationship Management (CRM) system. This approach serves multiple purposes: it ensures easy accessibility by eliminating time-consuming searches across various platforms, promotes consistency by offering a standardized set of resources to all team members, and allows for real-time updates that keep everyone on the same page. By placing everything at everyone's fingertips in one unified digital environment, we're streamlining operations, improving productivity, and fostering better alignment across all departments.

3. Inadequate Communication: If managers aren't involved in the strategy's early stages, they may feel blindsided and resist, not due to inertia but out of genuine concern.

The middle managerial layer, far from being an impediment, is often the backbone of successful transformations. They are the bridge over the chasm of change. As we'll discover in the subsequent chapters, if this bridge is wobbly, it might be due to missing supports from the top or turbulent waters at the bottom – but rarely is the bridge itself the problem.

Our team is committed to a culture of full transparency, making it a priority to keep every member informed about pertinent issues and statements that affect our day-to-day operations and long-term goals. We believe that open communication is crucial for both individual and collective success. To this end, we have established regular team meetings, updates, and open channels of communication where concerns, updates, and strategic shifts are openly discussed. Not only do we share what's happening, but we also delve into the 'why' behind every decision, creating a two-way street for feedback and questions. This practice ensures that every team member has a comprehensive understanding of the issues at hand and is empowered to contribute to solutions, fostering an environment of mutual respect and collective responsibility.

Navigating Change Resistance Through Radical Flexibility and Empathy

The evolving work landscape mandates a shift towards radical flexibility, placing empathy at the forefront of effective management. Recent data from a 2021 Gartner survey highlights a concerning reality: less than half of managers feel equipped to navigate this transformative paradigm. To truly thrive in this new era, managers must redefine their relationships with employees, positioning empathy not as a supplementary trait but as a fundamental management tool.

Historically, empathy has often been celebrated in leadership discourses but seldom prioritized in real-time managerial practices. An empathetic manager delves deeper than mere task oversight. They strive to understand the unique contexts in which their team members operate, asking probing questions that might reveal personal vulnerabilities and challenges. This approach goes beyond the surface level of performance metrics, focusing on the 'why' behind behaviors and decisions.

However, such a profound level of understanding necessitates a culture underpinned by trust, acceptance, and open dialogue. Managers are tasked with the delicate balance of eliciting candid responses without breaching trust boundaries, discerning the underlying motivations behind employee actions without resorting to assumptions, and harnessing the depth of socio-emotional intelligence to genuinely resonate with others' emotions. It's a challenging endeavor, but in an age where change resistance is prevalent, it's empathy that can bridge the gap, fostering an environment where adaptability and understanding reign supreme.

Traditionally, the role of managers has been overwhelmingly skewed towards reporting—keeping track of metrics, filing updates, and ensuring that the workflow aligns with company objectives. While accountability and structure are essential, this approach often fails to tap into the human elements of motivation, creativity, and morale, which are equally crucial for a team's success.

As a CEO, I've noticed that the most effective managers are those who see themselves not merely as overseers but as catalysts for change and inspiration within their teams. They understand that their role involves more than just 'managing'—it's about leading. Leadership, unlike mere management, cannot be captured in spreadsheets or PowerPoint slides; it's about inspiring your team, creating a vision, and then guiding your people toward achieving it.

The best managers know how to ignite the intrinsic motivation within their team members, sparking their natural desire to excel at their tasks and contribute to the organization's broader goals. This entails understanding what drives each individual—be it the joy of solving complex problems, the satisfaction of helping a client, or the excitement of pioneering a new process. When managers focus on fostering this type of motivation, productivity rises naturally, and reporting becomes a way to celebrate successes rather than a bureaucratic obligation.

I firmly believe that managers should empower their teams to make decisions within their areas of expertise. A culture that values autonomy and personal responsibility will encourage innovation and make employees feel more engaged in their roles. By allowing managers to focus less on micromanaging and reporting and more on guiding and motivating, we are liberating them to add real value to their teams and, by extension, to the company.

It's also important to recognize that motivation is not a one-size-fits-all proposition. What motivates one individual may not inspire another. Managers should adapt their leadership styles to meet the diverse needs and aspirations of their team members. This flexibility demands that managers become excellent listeners, empathetic mentors, and insightful coaches. They should also be able to communicate the larger organizational goals in a way that makes them relevant and attainable to each team member.

The evolution of managerial roles is a necessary response to our rapidly changing business landscape. Metrics and reports will always have their place, but they should not be the be-all and end-all of management. As we navigate through this era of technological change, globalization, and social shifts, it's vital for managers to concentrate on what truly counts: the human beings behind the numbers. In doing so, they elevate themselves from mere managers to true leaders—individuals who can inspire teams, foster innovation, and ultimately drive an organization toward a more promising future.

Navigating Change Resistance Through Empathetic Leadership: Nate's Journey

The changing contours of the business world present an ever-shifting challenge for managers and leaders. The pressures to evolve, adapt, and innovate while upholding the human side of operations are more pronounced than ever. And within this complex interplay between the past and the future, some leaders stand out with their ability to lead with empathy and resilience.

Nate: From Closer to Catalyst for Change

Nate's story in our company exemplifies this evolution in leadership. Moving 1500 miles away from familiar territory to manage an office with 20 associates was no minor feat. He not only had to grapple with the operational challenges of a new role but also had to shoulder the emotional and motivational needs of an entirely new team.

However, Nate's rise from a closer to an influential office manager was marked by an understanding that went beyond operational metrics. His leadership style consistently showcased his commitment to seeing beyond the obvious. Instead of being solely results-driven, he dug deeper, striving to grasp the unique circumstances and motivations of each team member.

Drawing insights from the 2021 Gartner survey, it's evident that the managerial community at large often feels ill-equipped to navigate the changing work dynamics. Yet, Nate stood apart, primarily because he didn't view empathy as an abstract leadership principle; for him, it was a tangible management tool.

Empathy became the lens through which Nate viewed challenges. When confronted with performance dips or unexpected behaviors, his first instinct wasn't to reprimand but to understand. By proactively inquiring about personal challenges or vulnerabilities that might be affecting a team member's output, he redefined the managerial-employee relationship, making it one based on trust and mutual respect.

Change resistance in management is, at its core, a byproduct of fear and uncertainty. However, under Nate's guidance, our company's new office turned into a haven of trust and adaptability. Instead of imposing a top-down change mandate, Nate wove change into the fabric of daily operations.

He recognized the value of open dialogue, ensuring that every team member felt seen and heard. This culture of acceptance paved the way for understanding the 'whys' behind decisions, fostering a climate where change was not just tolerated but embraced.

In a landscape where change is the only constant and resistance to it is a frequent challenge, the power of empathetic leadership shines through. Nate's journey is a testament to the potential of empathy as a potent tool for management. By embedding trust, understanding, and genuine concern into the heart of managerial practices, leaders can transcend traditional barriers, ushering in an era of holistic growth and adaptability.

CEO Perspective:

Certainly, navigating the complexities of middle management can be a challenging task for any CEO, especially when it comes to overcoming resistance to change. Here's how you could address this issue:

"In a dynamic business landscape, change is not just inevitable; it's imperative for growth. Yet, one of the most common challenges you'll face is resistance to change, particularly from middle managers who often serve as the conduits between upper management and frontline employees. While their resistance might stem from various sources—be it fear of the unknown, loss of control, or concerns about added workload—the role of the CEO is crucial in transforming this resistance into readiness.

Firstly, it's essential to be mindful of the unique position that middle managers occupy. They are the layer of management closest to the everyday operations and employee sentiments while also being accountable to the company's higher-level strategies. This duality can often make them the most risk-averse, as they have to manage both upward and downward expectations.

Engaging middle managers early in the change process can mitigate much of this resistance. Their input can be invaluable in foreseeing potential roadblocks and crafting strategies to overcome them. More importantly, early involvement fosters a sense of ownership, making them more likely to become change champions rather than change resistors.

Effective communication is also critical. Unambiguous, consistent messaging from the top can prevent a lot of the rumors and anxieties that naturally arise when change is on the horizon. Middle managers should be equipped with the information and tools they need to disseminate these messages to their teams accurately and constructively.

Empathy should not be overlooked. The human aspect of change—uncertainty, fear, and concern for the future—needs to be addressed openly. Allow middle managers the space to voice their concerns and ensure that these concerns are acknowledged and, if possible, addressed. Ignoring or downplaying their fears will only exacerbate resistance and could potentially lead to disengagement.

Finally, incentivize adaptability. In a climate where change is constant, agility should be rewarded. This could range from financial bonuses and promotions to public recognition within the company. When middle managers see that their efforts toward facilitating change are valued, they're much more likely to take ownership of new initiatives.

By taking a comprehensive, empathetic, and proactive approach, you can turn your middle managers into valuable allies in your organization's change management efforts. Remember, the goal isn't just to 'manage' resistance but to transform it into a driving force for progress."

The Indispensable Manager: A Catalyst for Employee Engagement and Organizational Success — A CEO's Perspective

It's an adage as old as management itself: "People don't leave companies, they leave managers."

Research, including polls by Gallup, substantiates this wisdom by pointing out that half of the workers in the U.S. leave their jobs because of their direct supervisors. Given these stakes, it's hard to overstate the importance of good management. Your managers are not just line supervisors; they are the lens through which employees see the entire organization. A subpar manager can rapidly erode workplace culture, leading to environments steeped in anxiety and mistrust.

When I talk about creating a culture of excellence, part of that is showing managers that their contributions are seen and valued. Highlighting their achievements in team meetings or company-wide communications serves dual purposes. First, it motivates the recognized manager; second, it sets a clear example for other employees to understand what excellence looks like in your organizational context.

However, when there's room for improvement, discretion is key. Public criticism not only harms the individual manager's morale but can also reverberate through their team, affecting overall performance and trust. Constructive feedback should be private, one-on-one conversations where the focus is on how to improve rather than what went wrong.

That said, we must distinguish between individual criticism and team learning moments. The latter can be invaluable. If a situation arises that everyone can learn from, sharing that situation as a case study can be powerful. It emphasizes that mistakes are not just individual failures but are collective opportunities for growth and improvement.

One of the fundamental shifts we need to make in modern management practice is to move away from the annual performance review as the primary feedback mechanism.

Managers, like anyone else, require continual feedback to grow and improve. Regular check-ins between senior leadership and managers and between managers and their teams create an ongoing dialogue that allows for real-time adjustments and fosters a more dynamic, responsive environment.

Managers should never be viewed as simply taskmasters or functionaries who exist to enforce company policy. They are coaches and mentors, critical to nurturing the professional growth of their team members. To perform this role effectively, they themselves need mentorship and support, which they should regularly receive from their superiors. By understanding where they need help or improvement, we can provide targeted training and professional development opportunities.

The role of a manager is multifaceted and of immense importance. An effective manager can uplift an entire team, driving productivity, fostering innovation, and ensuring employee satisfaction. Conversely, a poor manager can sink a team, causing not only high turnover but also eroding the quality of your products or services and damaging your brand's reputation. As a CEO, my focus has always been on cultivating a cadre of competent, compassionate, and visionary managers, for they are the keystones upon which the arch of organizational success is built.

Albert Sustainable Leadership

The skyline of the city was awash with hues of pink and orange as dusk approached. Inside Gorilla Inc, a different kind of transformation was unfolding. Albert, freshly inspired from a seminar on sustainable business practices, was eager to introduce initiatives that would make Gorilla Inc a pioneer in corporate sustainability. However, this task was more challenging than any software update or operational change.

Sustainability wasn't just about adopting a few green practices; it was a holistic shift in mindset and operations. Albert knew that for this to work, the drive had to come from all levels – from the top executives to the newest intern.

Albert initiated "Green Gorilla" – a campaign that would run for several months, focusing on different sustainability aspects. The kickoff was "Green Fridays." On these days, employees congregated in informal settings to brainstorm sustainable strategies and share personal green initiatives. They began with low-hanging fruits: recycling bins, digital documentation to reduce paper waste and energy-efficient lighting. But the ideas soon grew more innovative.

One team suggested partnering with local farmers to source organic food for the company cafeteria. Another proposed the installation of solar panels on the company's vast rooftop. Some even mooted the idea of "Green Holidays" – days off for employees to engage in community environmental activities.

Albert's role was not just to initiate but to ensure these ideas saw the light of day. He collaborated with different departments, secured budgets, and highlighted potential long-term savings and brand enhancement to the higher-ups.

The results were palpable. Energy bills decreased, employee morale soared, and Gorilla Inc even started attracting attention from eco-conscious clients. But more than any tangible benefit, the company's culture experienced a shift. Employees became more conscious of their actions, both inside and outside the office.

The media caught wind of "Green Gorilla," and soon, Gorilla Inc was in the headlines. The narrative wasn't about their core business but about their commitment to a sustainable future. Albert was invited to seminars and workshops to share his success story, turning him into an unlikely environmental ambassador.

Reflection: Sustainable leadership is more profound than implementing eco-friendly practices. It's about creating an ethos where every decision, big or small, is viewed through the lens of long-term sustainability. This chapter highlights the role of a manager in not just initiating change but nurturing it, fostering a company culture that goes beyond profits to consider the planet. Through Albert's journey, we understand that sustainable leadership is a blend of vision, perseverance, and the ability to inspire and mobilize an entire organization toward a common goal.

Chapter 3: The Role Of Target Outcomes

Change for the sake of change has often been the undoing of many well-intentioned strategies. Effective change is directed, purposeful, and outcome-driven. For an organization to successfully navigate the turbulent waters of transformation, clarity in desired outcomes is paramount. This chapter delves into understanding why target outcomes are essential and how they should be defined.

The Importance Of Clear Outcomes

Historically, many companies have jumped onto trends without fully understanding the endgame. For example, in the late 1990s and early 2000s, numerous businesses clamored to have an online presence. Yet, without clear outcomes, many dot-com businesses failed, not for lack of effort but for lack of direction.

Clear Outcomes Provide

1. Direction: Teams know where they're headed and can align their efforts accordingly.

2. Measurability: Success can be gauged, and course corrections can be made if the strategies in place are not leading towards the desired outcome.

3. Motivation: When the end goal is apparent, it energizes and motivates employees.

Financial Targets And Fundamental Change

Financial objectives, such as profit margins or revenue growth, are often primary drivers. But are they enough? When "Blackberry" dominated the market, they had excellent financial targets. However, the fundamental change driven by touchscreen smartphones caught them off guard. Their financial success masked the need for a more profound, more fundamental shift in product design and user experience.

Financial targets are critical, but they should be coupled with non-financial outcomes, like user experience, brand perception, and employee satisfaction. These factors play a long-term role in a company's viability and success.

Activities vs. Outcomes: Bridging the Gap

Merely being busy doesn't translate to progress. There's a significant distinction between activities and outcomes. Companies often get bogged down with metrics that measure activity rather than results.

For instance, "Blockbuster" was heavily focused on in-store rentals and late fees, metrics of activity. Meanwhile, "Netflix" shifted its focus to outcomes like user engagement and content variety, leading it to pioneer the streaming revolution.

How does a company ensure it's focusing on outcomes?

- Feedback Loops: Regularly evaluate and align activities with desired outcomes.

- Employee Training: Ensure that employees at all levels understand the difference between activity and results.
- Re-evaluation: Just as goals evolve, the outcomes may need to be adjusted based on changing market dynamics, customer feedback, or internal developments.

In the fast-paced world of the 21st century, having clear, well-defined outcomes is not just beneficial—it's essential. Companies that wish to not only survive but thrive need to have a clear sight of their destination. As the saying goes, "If you don't know where you're going, any road will get you there." The next chapters will explore the roles different organizational layers play in ensuring that the journey toward these outcomes is smooth and effective.

Harnessing Target Outcomes Through Empathetic Leadership

Refining the Role: Empathy in the Era of Target Outcomes

The post-pandemic era has heralded an intricate landscape for managers. Gone are the days when tasks and routine evaluations dominated their schedule. Today, amidst a blend of remote and in-person interactions, managers grapple with fostering team cohesion, ensuring task completion, and maintaining employee well-being. Amidst this juggling act, the crucial element of empathy is at risk of being overshadowed. But can we leverage the concept of target outcomes to aid this?

At the heart of a target outcome lies clarity of purpose. It defines what success looks like for a task or project. By intertwining empathy within the fabric of target outcomes, managers can create a more human-centric approach to achieving results. This means understanding the individual nuances of team members, gauging their comfort levels, and tailoring tasks that align with their strengths and personal circumstances. The result? Outcomes that resonate with both organizational goals and employee well-being.

While most management literature emphasizes the importance of communication, agility, and strategy, a quintessential element often gets less attention: the power of responsibility. Responsibility in a managerial role is not just an attribute; it's a force multiplier. Its impact reaches far beyond the borders of one's designated job description, touching every aspect of business—from employee morale and productivity to inter-departmental collaboration and, ultimately, to the company's bottom line.

Responsibility should not be confused with accountability. While both terms are related and often used interchangeably, they reflect different shades of ownership. Accountability implies an obligation to answer for actions or decisions; you might be accountable for delivering a project on time or adhering to a budget. Responsibility, on the other hand, is a proactive mindset, a willingness to take charge and make things happen rather than waiting to react to events.

The responsible manager is one who not only ensures that tasks get done but also sees the larger picture. This manager knows that their responsibility extends to shaping a positive work environment, mentoring employees, and aligning their department's objectives with the company's mission. They anticipate challenges, seek solutions before problems erupt, and act as a cohesive force within the organization.

The power of responsibility is transformational, and it is closely linked to motivation. When managers adopt responsibility as their guiding principle, they inspire trust and cultivate an environment that encourages open communication and creativity. This creates a virtuous circle, motivating employees to take ownership of their tasks and contribute beyond their primary roles.

Leading by example is one of the most effective ways to convey the value of responsibility. When you willingly take responsibility for both successes and failures, you set a precedent for the rest of the team. By showing that you are willing to own the outcomes of team efforts, you become a role model of resilience and leadership. This encourages a culture where team members also feel empowered to take the initiative without fearing blame or repercussions for genuine mistakes.

Responsible managers understand the power of autonomy. They do not micromanage; instead, they trust their team members and provide them with the resources and guidance needed to succeed. This shows that the manager is not only responsible for the output but also responsible for enabling each team member to contribute their best work. This heightened sense of responsibility cascades through the team, increasing overall motivation and engagement.

Responsibility doesn't end with your immediate team. The responsible manager also understands how their team fits into the larger organization. They build beneficial relationships with other departments, fostering a collaborative spirit that breaks down silos and boosts efficiency. The willingness to take responsibility for collective success and challenges extends to interactions with higher-ups, setting the stage for impactful leadership at all levels.

Responsibility is magnetic; it draws attention and earns respect. When decision-makers look for leaders, they often seek those who demonstrate a consistent commitment to responsibility. The manager who embodies this quality doesn't just tick off boxes; they contribute to the overall success and integrity of the organization. Therefore, it's no surprise that when promotions are considered, a strong record of responsible behavior can tip the scales in your favor.

Responsibility is the cornerstone of great leadership. It creates an atmosphere of trust, drives motivation, promotes a collaborative culture, and opens doors to career progression. By embracing responsibility, you can transform not just your management style but also the future of your organization. If you aspire to be a leader who leaves an indelible mark, make responsibility your guiding principle.

Reducing Managerial Burden: Paving the Way for Empathy

However, the road to empathetic leadership is fraught with challenges. Current managerial roles are bursting at the seams with responsibilities. With an overwhelming 70% of midsize HR leaders acknowledging this overload, a mere 16% have ventured to redefine the role of managers. This discrepancy leaves little room for empathy to flourish.

Take, for instance, the strategic move by leaders at Urgently, a pioneering digital roadside assistance entity. Recognizing the weight of maintaining team synergy in a predominantly remote setup, they recalibrated manager duties. By aligning team sizes to what managers could realistically handle, they created space for deeper, more meaningful interactions. This strategic rebalancing underscored the importance of quality over quantity, allowing managers to focus on high-impact relationships, thus cultivating empathy.

The Cautionary Tale of a Manager Losing His Way

The path from management to mere existence in the workplace is often a gradual one, barely noticeable until it reaches a tipping point. This chapter tells the cautionary tale of a manager who, despite being once engaged and motivated, slowly drifted into complacency and, eventually, into a personal and professional crisis.

John was a dedicated manager, initially driven by a commitment to excellence and team success. Over time, however, he lost that drive and began to see his job merely as a means to an end—a paycheck. As he withdrew, his responsibilities were subtly shifted to other team members, enabling him to slide further into the background.

Recognizing that his management position was no longer fulfilling, John made the decision to move back into sales, a role where he thought he could rediscover his passion. Unfortunately, his previous lack of focus had taken a toll. He failed to meet quotas and struggled with client relationships, displaying a lack of enthusiasm and skill that once characterized his work.

As his professional life unraveled, the repercussions began to affect his personal life as well. At the core of John's struggle was a yearning to be noticed and to find a meaningful connection, both professionally and personally. However, this deep-seated need for empathy and validation was not something that could be satisfied within the traditional boundaries of a career.

Feeling lost, John started acting out. Whether it was a missed deadline, an inappropriate comment, or a neglected responsibility, his behavior was a desperate cry for attention, but it went largely unnoticed in the busy workplace. By the time the severity of his situation was recognized, it was too late. John had lost his way, his position, and most tragically, his sense of purpose.

John's story serves as a sobering reminder that a paycheck alone is not enough to sustain one's drive and sense of fulfillment. It is crucial for both employees and employers to be vigilant about recognizing the early signs of disengagement. Moreover, this tale underscores the importance of providing emotional support and avenues for meaningful connection within the workplace—needs that, while not traditionally addressed in a career setting, are essential for overall well-being.

In any organization, the human element must never be overlooked. While businesses often focus on bottom lines and productivity metrics, it's crucial to remember that at the heart of every company are individuals seeking purpose, recognition, and a sense of belonging. Ignoring this can lead to not only a decline in professional performance but also personal crises, as epitomized by John's unfortunate journey.

The Future of Management: Empathy as a Cornerstone

As the world drifts towards hybrid working environments, the role of a manager evolves ever further. The intricate dance between achieving target outcomes and ensuring team well-being is a delicate one. To ace this, organizations must revisit the essence of management, shifting focus from sheer task completion to creating meaningful, empathetic interactions.

By addressing the trifecta of skill, mindset, and capacity, organizations can pave the way for an era where managers are not just taskmasters but empathetic leaders. Such a shift doesn't merely influence team dynamics but promises a robust return on performance in this redefined world.

Holding the Reins: Accountability and Performance Metrics for Managers — A CEO's Perspective

While a manager's influence can shape the organization from within, it is imperative to remember that they too, must be managed. Holding managers accountable isn't just about checks and balances; it's about creating a structured path for ongoing improvement and goal alignment with the organization's larger vision.

Accountability begins with clarity in expectations, often expressed as Key Performance Indicators (KPIs) or other measurable metrics. While soft skills like leadership and communication are crucial, hard numbers shouldn't be ignored. Sales growth, customer satisfaction scores, and employee retention rates are all quantifiable metrics that can offer a snapshot of a manager's effectiveness. The numbers don't lie, and keeping track of these metrics ensures that managers are consistently aligned with organizational goals.

I believe in the power of regular performance reports as tools for accountability. These reports, generated monthly or quarterly, offer a comprehensive view of a manager's achievements, struggles, and overall contributions to the company. Far from being punitive, these reports are collaborative documents that serve as starting points for discussions between executives or business owners and their managerial staff.

The key to making these performance reports effective is the dialogue that surrounds them. Executives or business owners should meet with managers to discuss the findings, offering both praise for accomplishments and constructive feedback for areas of improvement. These should be two-way conversations, where managers can also express any concerns they may have or resources they might need. This feedback loop is crucial for not only holding managers accountable but also for empowering them to succeed.

Sometimes, performance reports will highlight areas that need immediate attention or improvement. In such cases, corrective measures should be clearly outlined. Whether it's additional training, reassignment, or, in rare instances, demotion or termination, the path forward needs to be clearly defined and agreed upon. Importantly, these corrective steps should also be viewed as opportunities for growth, both for the managers in question and for the organization as a whole.

One often overlooked aspect of managerial accountability is the extent to which a manager upholds and propagates the company culture and values. Managers are culture carriers; their behavior sets the tone for their entire teams. Their alignment with the company's core values should be a significant part of their performance evaluation.

Holding managers accountable is a critical part of ensuring that an organization not only meets its current objectives but is also geared for future growth. A culture of accountability trickles down—when managers know they are held to high standards, those expectations permeate their teams and elevate the entire organization. This systemized accountability ensures that our organizational machine runs smoothly, with each cog efficiently playing its part.

Key Takeaways

Performance Reporting: The Foundation for Progress and Accountability

Performance reporting is more than a checkbox activity; it is the lifeline that sustains a culture of accountability, progress, and emotional well-being in a company. The process serves everyone from executives to managers to entry-level employees. It ensures not only that tasks are being accomplished but also that everyone is aligned with the company's mission and objectives. More importantly, well-executed performance reporting lets employees know that they are valued and noticed and that their contributions are critical to the company's success.

Why Performance Reporting Matters

For Employees

1. Tracks Progress: Consistent reports provide a road map of where you have been, where you are, and where you need to go.

2. Career Development: Enables you to proactively seek and engage in opportunities that will help you improve and grow.

3. Motivation: Knowing your work is recognized fuels motivation and fosters a sense of pride in your contributions.

Managers

1. Accountability: Regular reporting ensures that you remain accountable to your team and higher-ups for the projects under your purview.

2. Team Coordination: It helps you assess how well your team is working together and identify areas for improvement.

3. Resource Allocation: Effective reports let you understand where to direct resources, including time, budget, and labor.

Performance Reporting: Best Practices

Frequency Matters

Weekly or bi-weekly reports strike the right balance between too much and too little feedback.

Objectivity Is Key

Use data and specific examples to avoid ambiguity. Avoid using jargon and ensure that your metrics are universally understood within the company.

Two-Way Street

The best performance reports encourage dialogue. Employees should feel comfortable giving feedback, asking questions, and suggesting improvements. Do not focus solely on deliverables; consider soft skills like teamwork, communication, and problem-solving abilities.

Contrary to what some may think, managers are not there just to delegate tasks and hide behind emails and presentations. Leadership requires being present, not just in meetings but also in the day-to-day challenges that employees face.

The 'Walk-Through' Approach

Spend time on the floor, be it in a physical office or through digital platforms if remote. Know what your team is working on and what challenges they face. This shows you care but also serves as an implicit form of performance assessment. Do not wait for a quarterly review to address glaring issues. This only creates anxiety and saps morale. Open and honest communication is always better than formal rebuke.

Even with the most meticulous reporting mechanisms, the human element must never be forgotten.

Managers Should

1. Acknowledge Success: Never underestimate the power of a simple 'thank you' or 'well done.'

2. Provide Constructive Feedback: Help your employees grow; don't just point out their shortcomings.

3. Be Transparent: Share the big picture and how each role contributes to the organization's objectives.

In today's digital age, where it is easy to hide behind screens and superficial tasks, performance reporting brings us back to the fundamentals of business—real people achieving real objectives. Implemented right, it provides a nurturing environment where employees are motivated to be their best selves and where managers are not just overseers but active participants in the company's success.

By giving importance to performance reporting, you not only track progress and ensure accountability but also build a culture where everyone, from the intern to the CEO, feels they are a vital part of something meaningful.

CEO Perspective:

Certainly, establishing target outcomes is a pivotal aspect of managing managers, particularly when you're steering the organization through change or growth phases. Here's how you might elaborate on this topic:

"Setting clear, measurable targets is a proven strategy for ensuring team alignment and effectiveness. However, for managers, target outcomes serve a dual purpose. Not only do they act as performance metrics, but they also serve as a roadmap that can guide their leadership style and priorities. As a CEO, one of your key responsibilities is to establish these targets in a way that they become actionable blueprints for your managers to lead their staff.

The first step is to align these target outcomes with the company's broader strategic goals. Whether it's revenue growth, customer satisfaction, or innovation, each manager's targets should be a microcosm of the organization's macro objectives. This vertical alignment ensures that every team is working toward the overall success of the company rather than in isolated silos.

However, targets shouldn't merely be quantitative; they should also encompass qualitative aspects such as team morale, employee engagement, and customer relationships. These softer metrics often serve as leading indicators of long-term success and are directly influenced by the quality of management. Targets related to employee turnover rates, for instance, can serve as an excellent metric for gauging a manager's effectiveness in maintaining a motivated, cohesive team.

It's also crucial to establish regular review cycles for these targets—quarterly, semi-annually, or annually based on the nature of the objectives. These reviews offer an opportunity to assess not just whether the targets are met but also how they were achieved. Did the manager lead with integrity, foster a positive work environment, and inspire his or her team to reach these goals? Or were the objectives met at the cost of employee well-being and ethical considerations?

In addition, consider integrating adaptability into your target outcomes. The business environment is not static, and neither should your goals be. Managers should be encouraged and incentivized to adapt their tactics and, if necessary, recalibrate their targets in response to shifting circumstances, always in consultation with higher management to maintain alignment with overarching strategies.

Lastly, these target outcomes should not be set in stone but should evolve as your managers grow in their roles and as the company scales or pivots. The ability to meet and adapt targets should be part of an ongoing dialogue, one that informs future planning and organizational development.

By defining clear, aligned, and adaptive target outcomes for your managers, you're not just setting KPIs; you're giving them the tools and direction they need to lead effectively. Such a strategic approach to target-setting ensures that your managers are not just individual contributors but facilitators of cohesive, high-performing teams that drive the organization forward."

The Role of Target Outcomes: How I Discovered the Importance of Shared Endgames for Meeting Objectives

We've all been there—a quarterly meeting where objectives and targets are laid out in business jargon, greeted with a mixture of optimism and apprehension, only to be forgotten or misunderstood as the weeks roll on. In my early years as a CEO, I observed that despite setting what I thought were clear targets, there was often a significant gap between expected and actual outcomes. This led me to realize that for numbers to be met, endgames or target outcomes must be clearly articulated, understood, and internalized by everyone in the organization, from upper management to frontline staff.

The Revelation: It's Not Just About Numbers

My awakening came during a particularly challenging fiscal quarter. Despite having what I believed to be an exceptional product and a skilled workforce, we were not hitting our growth targets. Conversations with middle managers and team leaders revealed that while everyone was aware of the 'what'—the numerical targets—we had not adequately communicated the 'why' and the 'how.' This omission made it difficult for teams to align their daily activities with the larger objectives.

Numerical targets alone are abstract; they become meaningful only when translated into concrete actions. For instance, saying, "We need to grow revenue by 15%," is less impactful than breaking it down into specific initiatives like "introduce two new product lines" or "optimize the customer acquisition funnel for higher conversions." Upper management must work closely with middle managers to decompose overarching goals into actionable tasks that are clearly connected to the overall targets.

Once high-level goals are broken down into actionable tasks, middle managers act as the linchpin in communicating these to their teams. They need to provide context, helping team members understand how their individual contributions serve the larger objectives. This 'demystification' is crucial for fostering a sense of purpose and commitment, which in turn helps in meeting or even exceeding the numbers.

I discovered that when everyone in the organization understands the endgame, a sense of collective responsibility emerges. Teams become more proactive in resolving issues, more efficient in executing tasks, and more innovative in finding solutions. The role of upper management in this scenario shifts from micro-managing to enabling—providing the resources, information, and support required for teams to reach their targets.

Meeting targets is not a set-it-and-forget-it affair. Progress needs to be continually monitored, and this data must be transparently shared across the organization. I've found that periodic 'pulse checks' are invaluable for keeping everyone aligned. When teams are aware of where they stand in relation to the targets, they're more likely to be engaged in the process and take corrective actions as needed.

The experience of missing targets was, in many ways, a blessing in disguise. It forced me to reevaluate the way objectives were set, communicated, and pursued in the organization. I learned that for targets to be meaningful, they need to be broken down into actionable tasks, clearly communicated, and imbued with a shared sense of purpose. And most importantly, I realized that this cannot be a top-down directive but rather a collaborative effort where the role of middle management is invaluable. When everyone from the C-suite to the shop floor understands and buys into the endgame, not only are numbers more likely to be met, but the journey toward achieving them becomes a collective endeavor filled with purpose, engagement, and mutual accountability.

Implementing robust management practices begins with an introspective look at your existing systems. An audit can reveal the health of your current practices and indicate where improvements are necessary. This is an invaluable step that needs buy-in from both top and middle management, as their perspectives can offer a holistic understanding of organizational gaps and opportunities.

After gaining these insights, the next logical progression is to develop a comprehensive roadmap. This isn't merely an administrative task but a strategic initiative that outlines the specific actions, timelines, and resources required to bring your new management practices to life. Transparency is key here. Ensure that this plan is accessible to everyone it impacts so that each manager understands their role in the broader organizational transformation.

As you transition into the implementation phase, focused training sessions and workshops become crucial. Offering tailored educational experiences for both middle and top managers ensures that everyone is on the same page and equipped with the skills needed to succeed. These sessions act as a catalyst for change, embedding new knowledge and skills into the managerial DNA of your company.

However, even the most detailed plans and thorough training won't be effective without consistent reviews. In the early stages, frequent check-ins can identify friction points and offer opportunities for quick adjustments. Reviews should be dynamic, evolving based on the most recent outcomes and feedback. Speaking of feedback, it's imperative to encourage open communication throughout this process. Managers should feel free to share their experiences and challenges, whether in one-on-one meetings, team check-ins, or even through anonymous channels.

Before going all in, consider the value of pilot programs. By implementing your new practices on a smaller scale initially, perhaps within a single department or team, you can test their effectiveness in a more controlled environment. This minimizes risk and allows for data-driven refinements before a company-wide rollout.

As you begin to see success, celebrate it. Acknowledging and rewarding accomplishments, even minor ones, can generate momentum and reinforce the importance of adopting new practices. Conversely, don't ignore the setbacks. They are just as instructive, offering crucial lessons that can help refine your approach moving forward.

The process of implementing new management practices isn't set in stone; it should be fluid and capable of adapting to new challenges and opportunities. Always be willing to iterate, evolve, and fine-tune your strategies. This is especially important in today's fast-paced business landscape, where rigidity can be a liability.

Lastly, the role of internal champions cannot be underestimated. Identify those within your ranks who naturally align with the new practices and can serve as influencers. These champions can help expedite the adoption process by setting examples and encouraging their peers.

By carefully planning, communicating, and iterating, you'll do more than just implement new policies. You'll cultivate a culture that values excellent management at all levels—from middle managers who are closest to your workforce to top managers who define the company's strategic direction.

"Albert" The Pursuit of Precision: Albert and the Role of Target Outcomes

It was a rainy Tuesday when Albert walked into a meeting room filled with his managerial peers. They were gathered for a quarterly review, but Albert sensed an underlying tension. The company's latest strategic change initiative, though promising, had left many departments in a state of ambiguity.

After several presentations, Albert decided to take the floor. He began by acknowledging the promise and potential of the new strategy. But he also addressed the elephant in the room: the widespread confusion due to a lack of clear targets.

Albert illustrated his point with a metaphor: "Imagine a ship setting sail without a clear destination. The crew, however skilled, would be rudderless, leading to inefficiencies, overlaps, and conflicts."

He then introduced the concept of 'Target Outcomes.' He emphasized that while activities and efforts were essential, they needed to be tied to clear, measurable outcomes. These outcomes, he argued, shouldn't just be activity-based but should serve as beacons – shedding light on the broader strategic vision.

Albert Delineated Three Key Characteristics of Effective Target Outcomes

Outcome-Based Focus

Instead of merely focusing on tasks, emphasis should be on the desired result. For example, rather than just increasing sales calls, the outcome should be a tangible increase in conversions.

Financial Metrics

By aligning outcomes with financial targets, such as improving profit margins or revenue growth, departments could better prioritize their initiatives and resources.

Ambitious Yet Achievable

Target outcomes should push the team beyond their comfort zones but remain within the realm of feasibility. This balance would ensure motivation without overwhelming the teams.

Drawing from his own department as an example, Albert showcased how implementing target outcomes streamlined their workflow, eliminated redundancies, and fostered a sense of purpose and direction. By the end of his presentation, the atmosphere in the room had palpably shifted. There was a renewed sense of clarity, and managers were already discussing how to define and implement target outcomes within their teams.

Reflection: Albert's intervention at this crucial juncture underscores the pivotal role of clear target outcomes in driving strategic change. In the vast sea of corporate strategies, target outcomes serve as the North Star – guiding, aligning, and inspiring teams toward a unified vision. His approach is a testament to the power of precision and clarity in the intricate dance of corporate strategy and execution.

Outside the Box Insight to the New Generation

Generation Z: The New Workforce and the Quest for Loyalty

A new generation has arrived. Generation Z, those born between the mid-1990s to the early 2010s, are a force to be reckoned with. As they begin to make their mark in every sector and industry, businesses need to understand the nuances that make this generation tick. One of the key challenges for organizations today is to engage and retain Gen Z talent, ensuring they develop a loyalty and commitment to their jobs akin to what was seen in the 1950s.

Understanding Generation Z

The first step in harnessing the potential of Gen Z is understanding them. Growing up in an era of rapid technological advancement and global connectivity, they have witnessed firsthand the tumult of financial crises, political instabilities, and socio-cultural movements. This has made them pragmatic yet ambitious, digitally adept yet craving genuine human connection.

I Have Identified the Following Key Insights about Gen Z

1. Value-Driven: Gen Zers want their work to have a purpose. They are not merely looking for a paycheck but for a role that aligns with their personal values and passions.

2. Diversity is their Reality: Being the most diverse generation in the US, they expect and demand inclusivity in their workplaces. Discrimination and bias are deal breakers for them.

3. Digital Natives: This generation has never known a world without the internet. They expect workplaces to be technologically advanced and are quick to adopt new tools.

4. Work-Life Balance: Unlike the stereotype that they live online, Gen Zers value their offline time and seek a healthy work-life balance.

5. Seeking Stability: Witnessing economic downturns has made them value job security. They look for stability and growth opportunities in their roles.

Bridging the Gap: The 1950s and Now

The 1950s workforce, largely belonging to the Silent Generation and Baby Boomers, was characterized by loyalty and a strong commitment to a single employer. This was partly due to economic stability post-war and a cultural emphasis on job security. For them, success was defined by a steady job, a fixed routine, and gradual advancement.

To Foster Similar Levels of Commitment in Gen Z, Organizations Must

1. Align Values: Companies need to be transparent about their mission, values, and goals. Showing Gen Zers that their role has a direct impact can foster loyalty.

2. Promote Inclusivity: A diverse and inclusive workplace is non-negotiable. This not only attracts Gen Zers but also encourages them to stay.

3. Incorporate Technology: Modernize the workplace. Incorporate tools and platforms that facilitate collaboration, innovation, and efficiency.

4. Flexibility is Key: Offer flexible work hours, remote working opportunities and emphasize mental well-being.

5. Continuous Learning: Provide regular training and upskilling opportunities. This generation is keen to learn and grow.

6. Mentorship Programs: A touch of personal guidance can go a long way. Assign mentors to guide, counsel, and support them in their career journey.

As Generation Z steps onto the world stage, organizations need to shift and adapt. Understanding their unique perspective on careers and success and bridging the gap between old values and new aspirations is essential. With the right strategies, businesses can not only attract this new generation but also inspire loyalty and dedication reminiscent of the workforce in the 1950s.

Generation Z: The Workforce Evolution

Decoding Generation Z

As the curtains fall on the Millennial era, the spotlight is on Generation Z. Born between the mid-1990s to the early 2010s, their formative years coincided with rapid technological growth, socio-political upheavals, and economic downturns like the Great Recession. This backdrop has shaped their perception, behavior, and ambitions.

Defining Characteristics

- Pragmatic Dreamers: While their upbringing amidst economic challenges could have molded them into an extremely risk-averse group, Gen Z has shown an intricate blend of practicality with aspiration.
- Value Over Salary: The quintessential Gen Zer places significant importance on meaningful work. Salary, while crucial, is not the lone deciding factor for them. Their drive stems from a combination of personal interests and societal impact.
- Global Citizens: Having grown up in a connected world, Gen Z views global challenges, like climate change and social inequality, as personal ones. They align themselves with organizations that do more than just business.

The Implications for Employers

To cater to this emerging workforce, businesses need a drastic reorientation. Here's how they can make their environments conducive for Gen Z:

1. Commit to Societal Challenges: Being a responsible corporate citizen is no longer optional. Companies need to integrate sustainability and social responsibility into their core strategies.

2. Embrace Fast-paced Evolution In this dynamic age, businesses that remain stagnant risk obsolescence. They must be agile, always ready to adapt to the external environment's pace.

3. Redefine Career Paths: Traditional linear career trajectories won't suffice. Businesses should facilitate latticed career paths, allowing Gen Zers to explore diverse roles and develop varied skill sets.

4. Prioritize Training and Leadership Programs:" A keen emphasis on robust training is vital. These programs should resonate with Gen Z's values, especially emphasizing diversity and inclusivity.

5. Adopt Talent Innovatively: Traditional hiring practices might fall short. Instead, companies should:

Internal Apprenticeships: Cultivate talent from within, offering internships and apprenticeships.

Role-Fluid Hiring:" Hire based on potential and intellect, then find or craft roles that best suit the individual.

University Partnerships: Collaborate with educational institutions to tap into emerging talent, especially focusing on diversifying tech roles.

6. Skill-Matching Platforms: Setting up internal marketplaces can help align projects with the right skill sets, ensuring efficiency and job satisfaction.

7. Mentorship Programs: Harness the wisdom of previous generations. Gen X, Gen Y, and Boomers possess a wealth of knowledge that can guide Gen Z, shaping them into formidable leaders.

8. Reputation Management: In an age of online reviews and instant feedback, companies should be conscious of their image. A company's reputation, more than ever, has a tangible impact on attracting talent.

As Generation Z starts to dominate the workforce, understanding their intricacies is paramount for businesses. These young individuals bring a fresh perspective, blending pragmatism with a hunger for meaningful impact. For companies willing to evolve and embrace this change, the rewards will be manifold: a vibrant, committed workforce ready to lead the organization into the future.

In the midst of a rapidly evolving global landscape, Generation Z steps forth with a fresh perspective on leadership, reshaping traditional paradigms. Born amidst technological revolutions and societal upheavals, their worldview is distinct, shaped by their unique experiences and values.

Gone are the days when leaders stood atop hierarchies, issuing directives. Gen Z envisions leadership as a collaborative journey. They value a democratic style where decisions arise from collective insights, and input is sought from all echelons of the organization. This shift promotes a sense of collective ownership and responsibility.

For Gen Z, authenticity isn't just appreciated—it's demanded. They desire leaders who are genuine in their communication and actions. Transparency, especially in times of challenges or mistakes, fosters trust. In an age of information overload, leaders who can be forthright and sincere stand out. Merely chasing profits no longer suffices. Gen Z respects leaders who integrate a broader societal purpose into their vision. Be it climate change, social justice, or community initiatives, leaders are expected to leverage their influence for the greater good, embodying a purpose-driven ethos.

Digital technology is the playground of Gen Z. They don't just use technology—they live it. Consequently, they anticipate leaders to possess a degree of tech-literate acumen. While expertise in every evolving tech trend isn't obligatory, a fundamental understanding and a readiness to adapt are.

The tapestry of Gen Z is rich and diverse, and they naturally expect this diversity to be reflected and respected in leadership. This is not limited to mere representation; it extends to creating inclusive cultures, promoting diverse voices, and actively challenging systemic biases.

Leadership, in the eyes of Gen Z, transcends authoritarian boundaries. They yearn for mentors – leaders who guide, nurture, and invest in their holistic growth. Continuous learning, regular feedback, and a genuine interest in their aspirations become the cornerstones of this mentor-mentee relationship. Instead of compartmentalizing work and personal life, Gen Z seeks a seamless integration of the two. They value leaders who foster environments promoting mental well-being, flexibility, and the intertwining of personal passions with professional pursuits.

For Generation Z, emotional acumen is as vital as intellectual prowess. Empathetic leaders, attuned to the emotional landscapes of their teams, are held in high esteem.

Such leaders not only understand challenges but relate to them, fostering a nurturing work environment. In a digital age characterized by real-time feedback, Gen Z is naturally inclined toward results. They respect leaders who delineate clear objectives, provide regular feedback, and emphasize outcomes over rigid processes.

In sum, Generation Z's perspective on leadership paints a portrait of a holistic, human-centered, and adaptive leader. This leader isn't solely focused on guiding a team to organizational milestones but ensures that the journey is inclusive, innovative, and purposeful. As Gen Z begins to permeate the global workforce, their insights on leadership offer valuable lessons for organizations everywhere.

CEO Perspective:

Adapting Top Management To Lead Gen Z: The CEO's Perspective on Navigating Generational Shifts

As someone who has navigated through several shifts in the business landscape, one of the most significant changes I've encountered is the generational transition in the workforce. With the increasing presence of Gen Z in our ranks, it's clear that traditional approaches to management may not be as effective as they once were. It's not just about adapting to new technologies or market trends; it's also about understanding and embracing the unique perspectives and expectations that younger employees bring to the table. Here's what I've learned about adapting top management styles to better lead and engage with Gen Z.

First, it's crucial to understand that Gen Z has grown up in a different world from previous generations, and their priorities reflect that. They often value flexibility, inclusivity, and social responsibility over rigid structures, hierarchy, and pure profitability. For upper management, this requires a rethinking of company values and goals to better align with what motivates this new generation of workers.

Gen Z values authenticity and transparency, often seeking a two-way dialogue rather than a top-down approach to communication. As CEOs and executives, we need to foster an environment where these younger team members feel heard and valued. This means moving away from a "command and control" model and towards a more participative leadership style. It's no longer just about issuing directives; it's about engaging in meaningful conversations.

While Gen Z is incredibly tech-savvy, they also value genuine human interaction. They may prefer quick Slack messages for work updates, but when it comes to mentorship, career development, or problem-solving, they often seek a more personal touch. Top management needs to balance the use of digital tools with opportunities for face-to-face interactions, even in a remote or hybrid work setting.

Work-life balance and flexibility are not mere "perks" for Gen Z; they are often deal-breakers. This generation is looking for a more fluid integration of their professional and personal lives rather than a strict separation of the two. As a result, rigid 9-to-5 schedules and outdated notions of "face time" may need to be replaced by more flexible work arrangements that focus on productivity and results rather than hours clocked in.

Gen Z is incredibly focused on personal and professional growth. They are not looking to be static in their roles but are eager for new challenges and learning opportunities. Top management needs to offer more than just a job; we need to provide a career path with clearly defined growth opportunities, ongoing training, and mentorship programs.

The role of middle managers becomes even more critical when managing Gen Z. These managers serve as the bridge between upper management's strategies and the team's execution. Equipping middle managers with the tools and training to understand Gen Z's motivations can significantly improve communication, productivity, and job satisfaction across the organization.

The arrival of Gen Z in the workforce isn't just a minor blip; it's a significant shift that requires thoughtful adaptation from the top down. As CEOs and executives, we don't just set the strategy; we set the tone and the culture. Adapting our management styles to the expectations and aspirations of younger employees is not merely a tactical move—it's a strategic imperative that will shape the future of our organizations. In the ever-evolving business landscape, flexibility, openness, and adaptability are not just buzzwords; they are essential principles for leading a multi-generational workforce effectively.

Remote Realities: Managing Gen Z Employees in a Virtual World – A CEO's Guide

The rise of remote work has changed the employment landscape in ways we couldn't have imagined a few years ago. This transformation has been particularly relevant for Gen Z, who entered the job market as the most digitally savvy generation yet. While the virtual work environment offers numerous benefits, it also presents unique challenges for management—challenges that are accentuated when leading Gen

Z. Below are insights from my journey as a CEO on how to effectively manage remote Gen Z employees.

Let's start with the good news: Gen Z is comfortable in digital spaces. Their adeptness with technology means they adapt quickly to the tools that make remote work possible. But being a digital native doesn't necessarily mean one is effective at remote work. It's crucial to offer proper training and clear guidelines on how to use these tools not just for tasks but also for team collaboration and communication.

One downside of remote work is the potential for isolation, and while Gen Z might be digital natives, they are also deeply social beings. Maintaining a real, authentic connection is key. Use video conferencing for more than just meetings; consider virtual coffee breaks, team lunches, and one-on-one check-ins. Make it clear that despite the physical distance, every team member is a valued part of the corporate community.

Gen Z is highly motivated by clearly defined career pathways and objectives. In a remote environment, it's even more crucial to set explicit goals and offer a roadmap for how to achieve them. At the same time, this generation values autonomy. Remote work can actually facilitate this by focusing more on outcomes and deliverables and less on time spent at a desk. Use this to your advantage, but balance it with regular check-ins to provide direction and context.

Immediate feedback is a core expectation of Gen Z, influenced by instant gratification in social and digital platforms. Unfortunately, the remote work setting can sometimes delay feedback cycles. Counter this by implementing regular review sessions and instant messaging channels dedicated to project updates and acknowledgments. Remember, for Gen Z, no news is not good news; it's a vacuum that breeds uncertainty and disengagement.

Gen Z is incredibly focused on growth and development, but in a remote setting, there might be fewer opportunities for informal learning and mentorship. Consider setting up virtual mentorship programs and online learning courses specifically geared toward the career progression of your younger employees. Make it part of your managerial KPIs to track the progress of these initiatives.

Gen Z is more likely to be motivated by organizations that stand for something beyond the bottom line. This can be a bit tricky to communicate in a remote setting where corporate culture is less tangible. Regular updates on corporate social responsibility initiatives, diversity and inclusion efforts, and other value-based activities can help maintain engagement levels among remote Gen Z employees.

Managing remote Gen Z employees isn't merely about exploiting their digital fluency; it's about creating a work environment that leverages their unique talents while satisfying their career and personal aspirations. And while the challenges are unique, they're not insurmountable. They require a nuanced approach that respects their individuality while acknowledging the limitations and opportunities that come with a remote work setting. As CEOs and upper management, our role is to adapt and to provide leadership that not only manages but also inspires, regardless of where our team members are logging in from.

CHAPTER 4: MAXIMIZING LEADERSHIP POTENTIAL IN THE DIGITAL AGE

In the modern business landscape, with its ever-evolving challenges and opportunities, the role of leadership has never been more critical. Yet, a disconnect seems to be growing between what leadership offers and what organizations require. If the narrative of ineffective middle managers is misplaced, the lens must also turn toward leadership. How can we extract the most out of our leaders? And what does 'more' entail in the age of technology?

<u>Recognizing Leadership Inertia</u> is a task left loudly unspoken. Before we delve into solutions, we must address a prevailing issue: leadership inertia. It isn't always about leaders being complacent or lethargic; sometimes, it's about sticking with tried-and-true methods in an era that demands innovation. When "Yahoo!" faced stiff competition from Google and other emerging tech giants, its leadership clung to old models of online advertising and portal services, missing opportunities to innovate.

<u>Embracing Continual Learning</u> is what I preach. The tech age is synonymous with rapid change. Leaders must be at the forefront of learning and adaptation. Take "Satya Nadella" at "Microsoft." His emphasis on a 'learn-it-all' rather than a 'know-it-all' culture was pivotal in rejuvenating the company's innovative spirit.

<u>Cultivating a Vision Beyond Quarterly Earnings</u> is essential to success. Short-term financial targets are essential, but

leadership needs to envision the long-term picture. "Amazon's" Jeff Bezos often spoke about focusing on long-term goals, even if it meant sacrificing short-term profits.

<u>Facilitating Transparent Communication</u> is the key to growth. Leaders need to foster a culture where communication flows both ways. It's not about issuing decrees from the top but listening to feedback, understanding ground realities, and being approachable.

<u>Leveraging Technology for Decision Making</u> is a must! The digital age offers a plethora of tools, from AI-driven analytics to real-time data monitoring. Leaders must be adept at using these tools to make informed decisions. When "Domino's Pizza" realized its product was underwhelming, it used customer feedback data to revamp its entire pizza recipe, turning around its brand image and market share.

<u>Empowering Teams</u> in any business with a model of habit. Modern leadership isn't about holding power but distributing it. By empowering teams and individuals, leaders foster a culture of ownership, innovation, and responsibility. Adobe's move to scrap traditional performance reviews in favor of regular feedback sessions is a testament to empowering employees to take charge of their growth.

INVESTING IN PERSONAL AND ORGANIZATIONAL RESILIENCE

The technological world is fraught with disruptions. Leaders must cultivate resilience, both personally and organizationally, to weather failures, adapt to changes, and pivot when necessary. The resilience of Samsung after the Galaxy Note 7 debacle, for instance, showcases how strong leadership can guide a company through crises. Leadership in the technological era isn't just about navigating change but being at its helm. By fostering a mindset of continual growth, long-term vision, transparent communication, technological adoption, empowerment, and resilience, leaders can drive organizations to not just survive but thrive. The age-old adage remains true: As goes the leadership, so goes the organization. But in this age, it's about leadership that evolves, adapts, and, above all, leads by example.

Albert Maximizing Leadership Potential In The Digital Age

As Gorilla Inc. began to solidify its progressive ethos, Albert faced yet another challenge. The digital age was rapidly altering the dynamics of the business world, bringing with it a host of opportunities and challenges. And with it came the need to reassess leadership roles and strategies.

Albert, in his characteristic style, took the bull by the horns. He observed that while Gorilla Inc. had advanced digital tools and platforms, there was a disconnect. The leadership wasn't leveraging these tools to their maximum potential. Meetings were still long and inefficient, decision-making was protracted, and real-time data wasn't utilized for strategic planning.

Albert identified this not as a technological challenge but as a leadership one. The digital age demanded leaders who were not only tech-savvy but also adaptable, forward-thinking, and ready to break away from traditional hierarchies.

He initiated the "Digital Leaders" program, a rigorous training module that aimed at reshaping the leadership mindset for the digital age. It wasn't about teaching the leadership to use tools but to think, act, and lead digitally.

THE PROGRAM EMPHASIZED SEVERAL CORE PRINCIPLES

1. Agility: In an age where trends can change overnight, leaders must be nimble in their decisions and strategies.

2. Data-Driven Decision Making: The vast amounts of real-time data available should inform and guide leadership decisions.

3. Collaborative Tools: Using digital platforms to enhance collaboration, reduce bureaucratic lags, and make processes more transparent.

4. Digital Empathy: Recognizing that in a remote and digital work environment, human connections are still paramount. Leaders need to use technology to connect, not just command.

Albert led by example. He replaced his lengthy team emails with succinct video messages, making communication personal yet efficient. He started using analytics tools to monitor project progress and predict market trends, making his strategies more precise. Virtual town halls replaced conference room meetings, where team members from across the globe could share insights and feedback.

The results were evident. Decisions were swifter, strategies more informed, and the leadership team felt more connected to the ground realities of the digital age.

The digital age is not just a shift in technology but a shift in mindset. Leadership, traditionally viewed as a static role, now needs to be dynamic, adaptable, and digitally forward. Albert's journey in this chapter demonstrates that with the right approach, leadership potential can be maximized in the digital age. It's not about replacing the human touch with technology but enhancing it using the vast digital tools at our disposal. In the end, leadership in the digital age is about leading with clarity, agility, and humanity.

In today's technology-driven environment, marked by the proliferation of Artificial Intelligence (AI) and intense competition, measuring managerial effectiveness takes on new dimensions. The metrics have evolved beyond traditional Key Performance Indicators (KPIs) like revenue growth or customer satisfaction, although these remain vital. The challenge now lies in capturing a holistic picture that includes adaptability, technological savvy, and the ability to lead in an increasingly complex landscape.

Begin with the assessment of digital literacy. A manager's comfort and competence in navigating digital platforms, tools, and AI interfaces have become as essential as traditional leadership skills. They must not only be users but also advocates for the intelligent adoption of technology in daily operations. Gauge this through their utilization of existing tech tools, their willingness to undergo training, and their ability to influence their team's technological adaptability.

Look closely at how managers are driving innovation within their teams. Are they fostering a culture that rewards experimentation and tolerates calculated risks? In an age where disruptive technologies can change market dynamics overnight, the ability to innovate is crucial. It can be quantified by the number of new ideas generated, projects initiated, or even by less tangible metrics like increased cross-departmental collaborations aimed at innovation.

Another vital measure of effectiveness is data-driven decision-making. Managers should be adept at leveraging data analytics to derive actionable insights, be it for sales strategies, customer engagement, or operational efficiencies. Evaluate this skill by reviewing how often and how accurately data shapes their strategies and decisions and how effectively those decisions drive results.

Equally important is resilience in the face of setbacks and failures, especially those related to technological initiatives. Given the rapid pace of technological change, not every project will succeed. How managers react to these setbacks, learn from them, and pivot strategies accordingly is a telling measure of their leadership caliber.

Don't forget the importance of 'soft skills' like emotional intelligence, especially in an era when technology can sometimes overshadow the human aspect of work. Effective managers must excel at managing relationships, from their team members to their superiors and even external stakeholders. Tools like 360-degree feedback can offer invaluable insights into a manager's interpersonal skills and their ability to inspire, motivate, and lead.

Measuring managerial effectiveness should also take into account their adaptability to remote and hybrid work models, now a standard feature in many organizations. Look at how well they maintain team cohesion, morale, and productivity when not all team members are physically present. Metrics can include employee engagement scores, the quality of virtual communications, and the outcomes of remote projects.

In this technological era characterized by AI and intense competition, managerial effectiveness must be measured by a new set of standards. It's a complex blend of traditional leadership skills, technological prowess, and the intangible qualities that foster innovation and resilience. The spotlight is on their ability to merge technological literacy with emotional intelligence, to be as data-savvy as they are people-savvy, and to lead with a forward-thinking mindset that embraces both the challenges and opportunities that come with rapid technological change. By incorporating these multiple dimensions into your evaluation frameworks, you will not only measure but also cultivate managerial effectiveness fit for the modern age.

Chapter 5: The Interplay Between Leadership And Middle Management

In any organization, the relationship between leadership and middle management is pivotal. While leadership sets the course, middle management steers the ship toward the designated destination. But how does this dynamic work in the technological world, where adaptability is paramount and the pace is relentless? This chapter dives deep into the symbiotic relationship between these two essential tiers of management.

The success of leadership's vision is often contingent on middle management's execution. Conversely, middle management relies on leadership for direction and clarity. It's a dance of mutual dependencies, and when one stumbles, the other is affected. A classic example is "Nokia" during the rise of smartphones. Leadership was slow in identifying the changing market trends, and middle management, despite seeing the ground realities, struggled to pivot without a clear strategic direction.

Continuous, transparent communication is the lifeline of the leadership-middle management relationship. In organizations like "Tesla," Elon Musk's regular communications with all levels, including middle management, have ensured that everyone is aligned with the company's ambitious goals. By keeping channels of communication open, leadership can gain insights from the ground, and middle management can get the clarity they need for effective execution.

One of the defining features of successful organizations in the tech age is the degree of autonomy given to middle management. By entrusting managers with decision-making power, leaders not only reduce bureaucratic slowdowns but also foster innovation. "Google's" 20% time policy, where employees were encouraged to spend 20% of their time on projects they were passionate about, led to breakthrough products like Gmail and Google News.

For leadership to make informed strategic decisions, they require feedback from those in the trenches. Conversely, middle management needs feedback to ensure they're aligning with the company's objectives. Mechanisms for regular feedback, reviews, and course corrections can be instrumental. When "Microsoft" faced backlash for its Windows 8 UI, feedback from both consumers and its own middle management led to swift changes in subsequent versions.

A shared vision acts as a North Star, guiding all tiers of management. It's essential that leadership not only communicates this vision but also ensures buy-in from middle managers. When "Spotify" wanted to shift towards a more agile model, they ensured that the vision was co-created and shared, leading to the formation of their unique 'squads,' 'tribes,' and 'chapters' system.

The relationship between leadership and middle management is not just hierarchical; it's deeply collaborative. In the fast-paced technological landscape, it is this collaboration that determines an organization's ability to adapt, innovate, and succeed. As the old African proverb goes, "If you want to go fast, go alone. If you want to go far, go together." Leadership and middle management, in their collective stride, have the potential to not only determine the direction of their journey but also their monumental success.

Taming The Fire: A CEO's Guide To Managing The Angry Manager

It's an uncomfortable situation that every leader dreads: a manager within your organization is not just assertive but downright angry. Whether this anger manifests in hostile meetings, emails filled with exclamation marks, or confrontations with team members, it's a situation that cannot be ignored. An angry manager can severely impact the team's morale, productivity, and even mental health. As the CEO or an upper management executive, how do you manage this effectively? Here's my advice based on years of leadership experience.

Firstly, it's important to identify the root cause of the anger. Is it work-related stress, personal issues, or a toxic work environment that is causing such behavior? You can't treat the symptom without diagnosing the disease. Confidential, one-on-one conversations are a good starting point, but you might also consider bringing in a neutral third party like an HR representative or an executive coach.

Immediate Intervention

Tolerating an angry manager sends a message to the team that such behavior is acceptable. Immediate intervention is essential. This could be as simple as a private conversation where you make it clear that the behavior must change or as formal as written warnings and performance improvement plans.

In our organization, I take the emotional well-being and state of our managers extremely seriously, recognizing that their mindset directly impacts staff productivity. When a manager is angry or discontented, I address the issue immediately, prioritizing a face-to-face meeting to understand the root cause. This proactive approach aims to nip the problem in the bud, preventing any negative trickle-down effects on the team. The meeting serves as a safe space for open dialogue and constructive criticism, allowing us to find resolutions and alternatives to the issue at hand. By tackling these emotional disruptions head-on, we maintain a focused and harmonious work environment, ensuring that our managers are equipped to lead their teams effectively and positively.

Provide Constructive Feedback

When confronting an angry manager, the focus should be on constructive feedback rather than punitive measures. Point out specific incidents where their anger was detrimental to the team and provide alternatives for how they could have handled the situation differently.

It's not enough to tell someone to change; you have to provide them with the tools to do so. Whether it's anger management courses, stress relief training, or mental health resources, make it clear that the organization is invested in helping them improve.

Accountability and Follow-Up

Once you've addressed the issue and offered support, regular follow-up meetings are essential to track progress. Even if the situation seems to improve, don't let it fall off your radar. Continue to check in on both the manager and their team to ensure that the changes are having a positive impact.

To instill a culture of accountability within our organization, I hold daily meetings with key team members across various departments. These brief yet focused sessions serve as touchpoints to review the day's objectives, track progress on ongoing projects, and identify any roadblocks that need immediate attention. By making these meetings a non-negotiable part of our daily routine, I send a clear message that accountability is a shared responsibility and a cornerstone of our corporate ethos. This regular check-in keeps everyone aligned with our strategic goals and creates a sense of urgency, ensuring that tasks are not just delegated but are actually executed efficiently and effectively. The daily meetings act as both a spotlight and a support system, driving performance and encouraging transparency at all levels.

Which should be prioritized, accountability or responsibility? In leadership, this is more than a rhetorical question; it's a strategic choice that can profoundly impact an organization's culture and performance. From my perspective, the focus should unequivocally be on fostering a sense of responsibility, or ownership, among team members. When employees take genuine ownership of their tasks, they are inherently motivated to perform well, making it less likely they'll seek ways to manipulate the system.

Contrast this with a work environment where the emphasis is placed solely on accountability, often construed as a punitive measure. In such settings, the focus on metrics and results can eclipse the importance of employee engagement and personal responsibility. This approach can backfire, leading to high turnover rates and a culture of non-compliance. In the worst scenarios, employees may even resort to fudging numbers or cheating to meet imposed targets, thus defeating the purpose of accountability measures.

Good leaders understand the nuanced relationship between responsibility and accountability. They recognize that accountability, when used wisely, can be a valuable tool for guiding performance, offering constructive feedback, and facilitating improvement. However, they are keenly aware that accountability should not be used to intimidate or punish. Instead, it should serve as a framework for understanding performance metrics in the context of broader organizational goals.

It's essential that responsibility, or the taking of ownership, precedes the measurement of accountability. When leaders flip this equation, using accountability measures to impose responsibility, they are likely setting themselves up for failure. Employees, sensing the punitive nature of such an approach, may become disengaged or even resort to deceitful practices to meet expectations.

So, in summary, instilling a sense of responsibility first can create a virtuous cycle. Employees who take ownership of their work are naturally inclined to meet or exceed expectations, which then makes the application of accountability metrics a meaningful exercise for continuous improvement rather than a punitive measure. This balanced approach not only enhances performance but also fosters a culture of trust, empowerment, and mutual respect.

Evaluate the Team's Well-Being

Don't forget about the team that's been on the receiving end of this anger. They may require additional support or even training on how to handle difficult managers. Consider conducting anonymous surveys to gauge the team's morale or bring in a corporate wellness expert to offer coping strategies.

Despite your best efforts, there may come a time when it's clear that the angry manager cannot or will not change. In such cases, you must make the difficult decision on whether they can continue in their role. The well-being of the entire team and the broader organization should be the priority.

Managing an angry manager is a complex and sensitive issue that requires a balanced approach. The aim is to ensure that your intervention not only puts an end to the damaging behavior but also supports the manager in making positive changes. At the same time, the well-being of the rest of the team cannot be compromised. As a CEO or a member of the upper management, your role in resolving such issues is crucial, not just for the immediate problem at hand but for setting the tone of your organization's culture moving forward. After all, a ship is only as strong as its weakest link, and a turbulent manager can create ripples that affect the entire crew.

When managers fail to focus on the company's success, it creates a ripple effect that can reverberate through every level of the organization. No longer guided by a unifying vision, teams can become disjointed, and morale often declines. This lack of leadership turns the managerial role into a purely administrative one, void of inspirational energy and devoid of strategic intent. The long-term consequences for the company could be severe, ranging from missed business opportunities to a decline in market competitiveness.

As a CEO, when faced with managers who are not aligned with organizational goals, a significant pivot is required in leadership strategy. This usually involves some hard decisions—such as managerial reassignment, intensive training, or even termination—in order to reestablish a leadership framework that prioritizes the company's well-being. A thorough assessment is crucial to understand whether the issue lies in the lack of resources, insufficient training, or an inherent misalignment of values between the manager and the company.

To right the ship, senior leadership must reiterate the company's goals and values, clarifying any ambiguities that may have led to the misalignment. This often involves a transparent dialogue about what went wrong and why, followed by strategic sessions focused on realigning the team's objectives. Regular check-ins are necessary to ensure that the corrected course is adhered to and to identify any further adjustments that may be needed.

In the wake of managerial disengagement, a new emphasis on accountability becomes essential. This isn't about blaming but about establishing a culture where everyone—from upper management to entry-level staff—feels personally invested in the company's success. Leadership can facilitate this by introducing performance metrics that are directly tied to organizational goals alongside regular evaluations that hold managers accountable for their performance in relation to these aims.

In parallel, organizations should invest in identifying and nurturing potential future leaders who naturally align with the company's values and vision. Leadership development programs, mentorship, and rotational assignments are excellent ways to cultivate a new generation of managers who are not only technically competent but also deeply committed to the organization's success.

Neglectful or disengaged management is a challenge that tests the mettle of any leader. But it also provides an opportunity for adaptive leadership, offering the chance to recalibrate, reenergize, and revitalize the managerial framework. By taking swift, decisive action and realigning management's focus with that of the company, leadership can navigate through periods of uncertainty toward a future characterized by collective success.

THE DIPLOMACY DILEMMA: MANAGING THE OVERLY NICE MANAGER — A CEO'S VIEWPOINT

You might think an overly nice manager is a good problem to have. After all, who wouldn't prefer that to deal with an angry or confrontational manager? But as counterintuitive as it may seem, a manager who is too nice can also be detrimental to your organization's health. The inability to set boundaries, make tough decisions, or offer constructive criticism can lead to a lack of accountability, uneven performance, and, ultimately, an ineffective team. Here's my perspective on how to manage a manager who might be too nice for their own good.

Identifying the Challenges

Understanding the challenges that come with an overly nice manager is the first step. These challenges can include indecisiveness, a lack of authority, favoritism, and a reluctance to enforce company policies. Identifying these traits can help you target your interventions more effectively.

Start with an open and candid conversation. Frame the discussion around the manager's effectiveness and the impact of their niceness on team dynamics and performance. Make it clear that while a pleasant disposition is appreciated, their primary role is to guide their team effectively, which sometimes involves making tough decisions.

Fostering Emotional Intelligence

Being nice often comes from a place of high emotional intelligence, but this strength can become a weakness if not channeled correctly. Encourage your manager to use their emotional intelligence to discern when being nice is beneficial and when it's a hindrance. Workshops and coaching on assertiveness and leadership styles can be particularly useful here.

Provide training sessions that focus on key managerial skills such as conflict resolution, constructive criticism, and performance evaluation. Use role-playing exercises to help them practice how to handle difficult situations without compromising their integrity or the respect of their team members.

Balancing Empathy and Accountability

One of the most important skills to teach a manager who is too nice is the art of balancing empathy with accountability. They should be able to relate to their team members' challenges without letting them off the hook for their responsibilities. This balance is crucial for creating an environment where everyone feels supported but also knows that they are expected to perform. Continuing with this theme, training a manager who leans too far toward the "nice" side involves teaching the nuanced skill of blending empathy with accountability. Such managers often excel at creating an emotionally safe space, but they may falter when it comes to enforcing deadlines, setting expectations, or delivering tough feedback. The key is to equip them with the tools to be both compassionate listeners and effective leaders. During our training sessions, we focus on real-world scenarios that challenge them to be empathetic while also holding team members accountable for their tasks and commitments. Through role-playing exercises and open discussions, we explore the delicate balance of acknowledging a team member's challenges or constraints without compromising on the quality or timeliness of work. This helps create a work environment where staff feel both supported and motivated to fulfill their roles to the best of their abilities. The ultimate goal is to cultivate managers who can empathize with their team's struggles while simultaneously steering them toward excellence, ensuring that kindness does not come at the expense of performance.

Leveraging Peer Feedback

Sometimes, feedback from peers can be an eye-opener. If possible, set up a 360-degree feedback system where the manager can receive anonymized feedback from their peers and subordinates. This can offer invaluable insights into how their niceness is affecting their effectiveness. Just like with any other type of managerial challenge, regular check-ins are crucial. Use these opportunities to review how well they're applying the skills and lessons they've learned. Make any necessary adjustments and offer additional support or training as needed.

Sometimes, despite your best efforts, a manager's style might just not be the right fit for their role. It's important to remember that reassigning roles isn't a failure on anyone's part; it's about ensuring that every manager is in a position to contribute effectively to the organization's success.

An overly nice manager presents a unique set of challenges, but these are surmountable with targeted interventions, training, and ongoing support. As a CEO or a member of upper management, your responsibility isn't just to manage people but to lead them — to help them become the best versions of themselves for the benefit of the entire organization.

So, don't shy away from the issue. Address it head-on and turn what could be a potential weakness into an organizational strength.

CEO Perspective:

From a CEO's vantage point, the relationship between leadership and middle management is much like the interplay between the brain and the nervous system in the human body. The top leadership, or the 'brain,' sets the strategic direction, formulates policies, and establishes organizational goals. In contrast, middle management acts as the 'nervous system,' transmitting these directions into actionable tasks while providing crucial feedback to adapt and fine-tune strategies. The success of an organization, particularly in volatile business landscapes, depends largely on how well these two tiers of management interact and collaborate.

Firstly, it's essential to understand that middle managers are often the custodians of organizational culture. They are closer to the front lines, interacting daily with individual contributors. They understand the pulse of the organization: what motivates the staff, what challenges they face, and how well they align with the company's objectives. As a CEO, tapping into this treasure trove of insights can make the difference between a decision that is merely good and one that is truly great. It requires an open channel of communication and a culture that encourages upward feedback without fear of reprisal.

Secondly, middle managers are crucial change agents. When a new strategy or technological tool is introduced, they are usually the ones responsible for its implementation at the ground level. Their buy-in is essential not just for a smooth rollout but also for long-term adoption. Hence, involving middle managers in the decision-making process, especially when significant changes are planned, can preempt resistance and foster a more accepting organizational climate. The dialogue between leadership and middle management should be bidirectional: top-down when it comes to strategic direction and bottom-up for feedback and tactical considerations.

In today's fast-paced, tech-centric world, agility is a coveted asset. Middle managers can be instrumental in imbuing the organization with this quality. They can quickly adapt to market changes, implement new processes, and pivot strategies as required, but only if they are empowered by top leadership to do so. An agile organization is characterized by its flattened hierarchies, open channels of communication, and a propensity for rapid, data-informed decision-making, and middle managers are pivotal in bringing this agility to life.

Equally important is the development and training of middle managers. They are the leadership pipeline, the future executives who will one day steer the ship. A CEO must invest in their growth not just to increase their effectiveness in their current roles but also to prepare them for more significant responsibilities down the line. This involves targeted training programs, mentorship opportunities, and even cross-functional projects that broaden their perspective and sharpen their skill sets.

Ultimately, the relationship between top leadership and middle management should be a symbiotic one, each enhancing the effectiveness of the other. By creating an organizational framework that promotes seamless collaboration between these two crucial layers, CEOs can better position their companies for enduring success in today's complex, dynamic business environment.

As a CEO, consider your middle managers as partners in the enterprise, essential both for implementing your vision and for providing the insights and feedback that can make that vision more achievable and impactful. Your organization's strength lies in the sum of its parts, and a strong, synergistic relationship between leadership and middle management is key to unlocking that strength.

NAVIGATING THE LABYRINTH OF LEADERSHIP AND MIDDLE MANAGEMENT DYNAMICS

In the tech ecosystem, where trends evolve rapidly, there's a risk that leadership may fall out of touch with the latest technologies or methodologies. Middle management, being closer to daily operations, can play a pivotal role in bridging this knowledge gap. "Adobe," for instance, successfully made the transition from selling packaged software to cloud-based subscription services, a massive shift that was facilitated by insights and expertise from middle managers well-acquainted with the changing dynamics of software consumption.

While traditionally, mentorship is viewed as a top-down process, a two-way mentorship can be immensely beneficial. Leaders can provide middle managers with insights into strategic decision-making and broad-scale thinking. Conversely, middle managers can offer leaders a fresh perspective, updating them about new tools, technologies, and tactics they might be unaware of. At "Salesforce," their mentoring program allows this two-way flow of information, ensuring that both leadership and middle management are continuously learning from each other.

In many organizations, feedback is viewed with apprehension, often seen as criticism. However, companies that have thrived in the technological era have cultivated an environment where feedback, both upwards and downwards, is encouraged and valued. By instilling a feedback-positive culture, organizations like "Netflix" have maintained their agility. Their feedback-rich environment, devoid of unnecessary bureaucracy, allows for swift decisions, adaptations, and innovations.

The true test of the bond between leadership and middle management often comes in times of crisis. When challenges arise, this bond becomes the organization's bedrock. A case in point is "Samsung" during the Galaxy Note 7 crisis. Leadership set the tone by taking responsibility, while middle management was instrumental in handling the logistics of recalls, customer communications, and swift redesigns. Their coordinated response turned a potential PR disaster into a testament to their resilience.

Innovation is not the sole domain of any single tier of management. When leadership and middle management collaborate with a unified purpose, innovation thrives. "Apple," under the combined vision of Steve Jobs and his dedicated team of middle managers and engineers, continuously pushed the boundaries of what was possible, leading to revolutionary products like the iPhone and iPad.

The intricate dance between leadership and middle management is the heartbeat of any thriving organization. It's a relationship built on mutual respect, continual learning, and a shared mission. As technology continues to evolve, it's this partnership that will guide organizations, allowing them to pivot with grace, innovate with purpose, and surge ahead with unmatched momentum. In this dynamic interplay lies the future of organizational success in the tech age.

Building the Mindset

Cultivating an owner's mindset among managers is paramount for a thriving company. It begins with entrusting them with significant decisions. When managers sense this deep trust and feel they can directly influence outcomes, they naturally align with the company's long-term vision. This alignment is further reinforced when the organization's mission, values, and overarching goals are consistently communicated. Understanding the broader perspective ensures that every decision made resonates with the company's objectives.

Financial incentives, such as profit-sharing or stock options, can also play a pivotal role. A direct financial stake in the company's trajectory instigates an intrinsic motivation to see the business succeed. Celebrating achievements, both big and small, goes a long way too. Whether through financial rewards, promotions, or heartfelt commendations, recognizing exemplary work can significantly boost a manager's dedication and sense of purpose.

Inclusivity is another key facet. Creating an environment where managers freely voice their thoughts, concerns, and insights not only provides fresh perspectives but also strengthens their sense of belonging and importance. Parallelly, investing in continuous learning and professional development opportunities can deepen this commitment. When managers see a clear growth trajectory within the company, their engagement and dedication naturally amplify.

Promoting innovative thinking by organizing brainstorming sessions or platforms for managers to pitch novel business ideas can also stimulate a proactive, owner-like mindset. While empowerment forms the bedrock of this approach, it's vital to maintain checks and balances. Establishing clear responsibility metrics ensures that managerial decisions remain aligned with company objectives and standards.

Equipping managers with the necessary tools, resources, and training is indispensable. Not only does this empower them to make informed decisions, but it also underscores the company's commitment to their roles. Complementing this with a culture that champions inter-departmental collaboration can further encourage managers to adopt a holistic, company-wide approach to their tasks.

In weaving these elements together, an organization can effortlessly instill an owner's mindset among its managers, ensuring they act with foresight, passion, and a deep-rooted commitment to the company's ethos and success.

Now, let's take a look at the Impact of Leadership Styles on Employee Retention.

Leadership, often perceived as the driving force behind an organization's success, also profoundly influences the subtle nuances of the workplace. One of these nuances is employee retention, which hinges heavily on the relationship between leaders and their teams. When we navigate the labyrinth of leadership styles, it becomes evident that each style carries with it a unique set of implications for employee longevity.

Transformational leaders, with their ability to inspire and motivate through a shared vision, often cultivate environments where employees feel valued and engaged. Such workplaces invariably witness heightened job satisfaction, making employees less inclined to seek opportunities elsewhere.

On the other hand, "transactional leadership," grounded in clear structures and performance-based rewards or penalties, offers a mixed bag. While some employees relish the clarity and direct reward systems, others might find it stifling. The risk here lies in an overemphasis on penalties or an overly bureaucratic approach that can dampen the spirit of innovation and autonomy.

The "autocratic style," where leaders rule with an iron fist, making decisions unilaterally, can be a deterrent to retention. Such environments might see dwindling morale as employees grapple with feelings of disempowerment.

Conversely, "laissez-faire leaders" who adopt a hands-off approach grant their employees a significant degree of decision-making power. While many professionals might thrive under such autonomy, there's a segment that could feel rudderless, craving direction and clearer expectations.

A leadership style that often garners positive feedback is "servant leadership." By prioritizing the needs of the team and focusing on their development, these leaders foster environments characterized by cohesion, job satisfaction, and loyalty.

Lastly, democratic or participative leaders who weave their teams into the decision-making fabric often cultivate workplaces where employees feel heard, valued, and engaged. This sense of inclusivity can be a potent tool for retention.

Crafting a Retentive Environment

Beyond identifying leadership styles, it's imperative to understand how these styles can be harnessed or tweaked to influence retention positively. Job satisfaction isn't merely about remuneration or job roles. It extends to feeling supported, valued, and being part of a broader organizational vision. Leadership that underscores these aspects can create a sticky factor for employees. One of the strongest retentive tools is the promise of growth. Leadership that emphasizes mentoring, continuous learning, and opportunities for advancement gives employees compelling reasons to stay. The tone set by leadership shapes organizational culture. An environment that champions positivity, inclusivity, and transparency becomes a magnet for talent. The essence of strong leadership lies in its ability to communicate. Open channels, transparent dialogues, and trust-building conversations can fortify bonds between leaders and their teams.

Beyond the direct influence of leadership styles, there's a broader narrative at play. Today's workforce, particularly the younger generation, seeks more than just a paycheck. They crave purpose, meaning, and an alignment of values. It's here that leadership must step in, not only to demonstrate strong work ethics but also to weave them into the organization's tapestry. By giving employees a reason, a cause to rally behind, leaders can instill a sense of purpose. Whether it's sustainability, community welfare, innovation, or any noble cause, having a clear organizational mission can resonate with employees, giving them a reason to commit and stay.

Leadership isn't a one-size-fits-all proposition. It's a dynamic, evolving paradigm that demands adaptability, empathy, and a keen understanding of the human psyche. As organizations grapple with the challenge of retention, it's evident that the answer lies not just in strategies and policies but in the very essence of leadership.

The Ripple Effect: Leading Leaders

A leader's influence is most profoundly felt when it ripples through an organization's tiers. This influence is not just about inspiring the broader workforce; it often begins closer to home, with fellow leaders and managerial peers. The dynamic between leaders is pivotal, for when leaders influence and inspire one another, the effects cascade down the organization's hierarchy, amplifying their collective impact.

It's a fundamental truth that to inspire an entire organization, there must first be harmony, alignment, and motivation at the leadership levels. When one leader can positively influence another, the combined effect on the broader team is magnified. This is because leaders, by virtue of their roles, have their own spheres of influence. A single unified message or vision, when propagated by multiple aligned leaders, reaches the workforce with reinforced vigor and clarity.

At the core of a leader's ability to influence is their own motivation. A motivated leader is not just an individual with a vision but someone fueled by passion, purpose, and an unwavering commitment to the cause. However, leaders, like all individuals, can experience periods of diminished motivation. It is in these moments that the interconnected fabric of leadership within an organization proves its worth.

A cohesive leadership team can rally around one of their own, reigniting the spark of motivation. This mutual support system, where leaders uplift and inspire one another, ensures that the organization never lacks direction, even in challenging times.

Persuasion is an intrinsic part of leadership. But to persuade others, a leader must first be wholly convinced and passionate about the cause. This authenticity is palpable and is often the difference between mere compliance and genuine commitment from the team.

Persuasion is not about dictating but rather presenting a compelling vision that others want to be part of. For instance, understand the concerns, objections, and perspectives of fellow leaders and team members. Recognize and validate the feelings and viewpoints of others, even if they diverge from one's own. Clearly articulate the objectives, benefits, and the bigger picture. Demonstrating commitment, work ethic, and passion in one's actions, which often speaks louder than words.

The dynamics of leadership extend beyond the individual. It's an interconnected dance where leaders influence one another, drawing strength, motivation, and inspiration from their peers. As they align, their combined influence permeates the organization, creating a culture of motivation, unity, and purpose. It's a reminder that leadership is not a solitary journey but a collective endeavor, where the whole is indeed greater than the sum of its parts.

"Albert" the Interplay Between Leadership and Middle Management

As the winter months rolled in, Albert found himself grappling with a new challenge at Gorilla Inc. While the various initiatives he'd spearheaded had rejuvenated the organization's ethos, there was a subtle yet unmistakable tension brewing between the top leadership and the middle management.

Albert recognized this as a challenge many corporations face: The visionaries at the top set forth grand strategies, while the middle managers, like himself, are tasked with translating these visions into actionable plans. Often, the practicalities and nuances at the ground level are overlooked or miscommunicated, leading to friction.

The first signs of this interplay came during a quarterly review meeting. The leadership introduced a new product line, expecting it to be rolled out in the next quarter. But the timelines seemed unrealistic to Albert and his peers. The product required extensive research, testing, and market analysis. However, when these concerns were raised, they were brushed off. The leadership felt the middle management was resistant to change, while the managers felt their hands-on knowledge was undervalued.

Albert, always the problem solver, took it upon himself to bridge this gap. He proposed the "Confluence Conventions" - monthly forums where leadership and middle management would congregate not as superiors and subordinates but as collaborators.

In the first Confluence Convention, Albert took the stage and presented a unique visualization. He depicted the company as a ship. The leadership was the compass, providing direction. The middle management and teams were the rudders and sails, guiding the ship based on the compass's direction. Both were essential. A compass without a rudder is aimless, and a rudder without a compass is directionless.

The convention was structured innovatively. Leaders would present their visions, after which managers would brainstorm how to bring these visions to life. This wasn't a space for confrontation but collaboration. Managers provided ground-level insights, potential challenges, and actionable timelines. Leaders, in turn, provided broader perspectives, market outlooks, and resources.

Over time, these conventions transformed the dynamics of Gorilla Inc. Strategies were more aligned, projects more successful, and most importantly, the respect between leadership and middle management grew exponentially.

Reflection – the interplay between leadership and middle management is a delicate dance, one that determines the rhythm of an organization. Through Albert's initiative, we understand that for a company to truly succeed, it's essential to value the compass and the rudder equally. Both bring unique strengths, insights, and value to the table. And when they work in harmony, the ship doesn't just sail; it conquers uncharted waters. This chapter highlights the importance of dialogue, respect, and collaboration in achieving organizational excellence.

Chapter 6: Beyond Monetary Motivations: Providing Clarity and Direction

In an increasingly competitive and technologically driven business landscape, understanding what truly motivates employees and managers is paramount. Historically, compensation has been the go-to lever for many organizations aiming to drive performance. Yet, as underlined in the seminal book "Money Doesn't Motivate," there's a growing recognition that monetary incentives alone aren't the silver bullet for motivation. This chapter delves into the importance of clear direction and standards in motivating managers and, by extension, their teams, drawing insights from the aforementioned text and juxtaposing it against the backdrop of modern management practices.

The Myth Of Monetary Motivation

The book "Money Doesn't Motivate" challenges the traditional notion that higher compensation directly translates to better performance. While fair compensation is undoubtedly essential, it's not always the primary driver for managers and employees. Research shows that once individuals reach a certain income level, their motivation to excel often stems from non-monetary factors.

One of the most potent motivational tools for managers is clarity in expectations and goals. When managers have a clear understanding of what's expected of them, they can better strategize, prioritize, and lead their teams. For instance, companies like "Atlassian" and "Zappos" emphasize clarity in their organizational missions, which helps align teams toward common goals.

Beyond clarity, setting high but achievable standards pushes managers to excel. These standards become benchmarks that drive excellence throughout the organization. Firms like "Toyota" with their lean manufacturing principles or "Four Seasons" in the hospitality industry, exemplify the impact of setting and adhering to high standards.

While clarity and standards are vital, it's equally crucial to trust managers with the autonomy to achieve these standards in their own way. Micromanagement can stifle creativity and impede innovation. By contrast, companies like "3M" have seen immense success by trusting their employees with autonomy, leading to innovations like the Post-it Note, born out of the company's allowance for "free time" projects.

Recognition of achievements and providing avenues for growth can be more motivating than monetary bonuses. Recognizing and celebrating successes, no matter how big or small, fosters a culture of appreciation. Additionally, providing opportunities for personal and professional growth ensures that managers see a clear path ahead. "Goldman Sachs," for instance, has been renowned for its rigorous training and development programs, ensuring that its employees are continually growing and evolving.

Regular, constructive feedback can guide managers more effectively than sporadic monetary bonuses. A culture where feedback is viewed as a tool for growth rather than criticism can propel managers to continuously improve. Companies like "Adobe," which transitioned from traditional annual reviews to regular feedback sessions, have reported more engaged and motivated teams.

As we glean from "Money Doesn't Motivate" and myriad real-world examples, while compensation is essential, it's just one facet of motivation. In the ever-evolving world of business, it's the combination of clear directions, high standards, autonomy, recognition, growth opportunities, and valuable feedback that truly drives managers and their teams toward excellence. When these elements coalesce, they create an environment where motivation thrives beyond the paycheck, leading to sustained organizational success.

Essentials for Managers in a Rapidly Evolving Landscape

The complex role of managers, especially in our current technological and fast-paced environment, cannot be underestimated. They are the bridge between leadership and the workforce, charged with translating vision into actionable steps and ensuring those steps are executed effectively. Let's delve further into what managers truly need to succeed in this capacity.

For managers to steer their teams in the right direction, they first need to understand where the company is headed. When leadership provides a well-articulated vision for the future, managers can align their departmental goals accordingly. For example, when "Satya Nadella" took over as CEO of Microsoft, he imparted a clear vision of a "mobile-first, cloud-first" world. This clarity enabled managers across the company to align their strategies and resources effectively.

Providing managers with the right resources, whether it's manpower, technology, or training, is crucial. A manager, no matter how competent, will flounder without the necessary tools to do their job. Companies like "Slack" and "Zoom" have transformed workplace communication, offering managers tools to streamline workflows and enhance collaboration.

The technological world is in a state of constant flux. What's relevant today might be obsolete tomorrow. Managers need ongoing training and development opportunities to stay abreast of the latest in their field. "Amazon's" Leadership Principles workshops offer their managers a chance to continually refine their leadership skills and understand the company's evolving ethos.

Managers need to feel supported by the higher-ups. This doesn't just mean having resources; it means having leaders who are approachable, willing to listen, and open to feedback. The open-door policy adopted by many leading organizations, such as "Southwest Airlines," has proven successful in fostering a culture where managers feel their concerns are heard and addressed.

Just as managers are expected to provide feedback to their team members, they, too, need feedback on their performance. Constructive feedback, both from their superiors and their teams, can help managers identify areas of improvement. Organizations like "General Electric," with their continuous performance development process, emphasize the importance of ongoing dialogue over annual reviews.

Burnout is a genuine concern, especially in high-stress managerial roles. Companies that recognize the importance of work-life balance tend to have more satisfied, productive, and long-serving managers. "Netflix's" unlimited vacation policy, while seemingly radical, underscores the company's trust in its employees to make decisions in the best interest of both their personal lives and the company.

While the earlier discussion, "Money Doesn't Motivate," highlights that money isn't the sole motivator, recognition plays a pivotal role in manager motivation. Knowing that their efforts are seen and appreciated can spur managers to even greater heights. Tech giants like "Google" employ various recognition programs, celebrating everything from significant milestones to innovative ideas, ensuring their managers feel valued.

Managers are a linchpin in the organizational machinery. By understanding their unique needs and ensuring they are met, companies can create a thriving environment where managers not only excel in their roles but also drive their teams towards overarching organizational goals. In the nuanced dance of business success, attending to the needs of these vital players is non-negotiable.

CEO Perspective:

As a CEO, I've often found that a lucrative salary or a generous bonus is not enough to keep a manager fully engaged in their role. Although financial rewards are important, they are not the be-all and end-all of motivation. It's the intangibles—clarity, direction, and a sense of purpose—that elevate a manager's job from a mere occupation to a fulfilling career.

From my vantage point, clarity is one of the most invaluable assets I can provide to my management team. In a world where business complexities are ever-increasing, having a clear vision and transparent objectives reduces uncertainty and empowers managers to make confident decisions. For me, this means frequent and open communications, whether through regular town halls, one-on-one meetings, or company-wide memos. I aim to clarify organizational goals, delineate how each department fits into the larger picture, and articulate what success looks like on both a company and individual level. When managers have a clear understanding of what is expected and why, they are more likely to be engaged and effective in their roles.

Direction complements clarity. While clarity outlines the 'what' and the 'why,' direction gives insight into the 'how.' As the CEO, my role is not just to set the destination but also to provide a roadmap. This may involve briefing managers on market trends, technological advancements, and competitive landscapes. It's about laying out strategic pathways and helping them understand the shifting terrains of the business world. I invest in regular strategy sessions and encourage an open dialogue for troubleshooting, brainstorming, and fine-tuning our approaches. Managers, when equipped with this level of guidance, feel more secure, less anxious about the unknown, and more adept at steering their teams through challenges.

But even clarity and direction can fall flat without a compelling sense of purpose. Financial gains are often short-lived motivators, but the purpose is enduring. It's what makes managers and their teams go the extra mile, even when no one is watching. I believe in consistently connecting the dots between day-to-day operations and our broader mission. This can be as simple as sharing customer testimonials that demonstrate the impact of our work or as elaborate as community outreach programs that align with our company values. When managers see that their efforts have a meaningful impact, it fosters a sense of pride and a deeper connection to their work.

To sum it up, as a CEO, I view my role as a provider of more than just monetary rewards. I am the custodian of the company culture, the clarifier of vision, and the navigator of our corporate journey. By offering clarity, setting direction, and instilling a sense of purpose, I aim to cultivate a motivated, engaged, and high-performing management team that is equipped to lead in an increasingly complex business environment.

Hidden Leaders: Unearthed Assets in Building an Ownership Culture

In every organization, amidst well-defined hierarchies and titles, there exists a unique breed of individuals—hidden leaders. These individuals may not always have the grandest titles or the most prominent roles, but their actions, mindset, and influence reverberate deeply within the company's culture. They are the unsung heroes who champion the organization's ethos, drive initiatives with genuine passion, and often influence their peers in profound ways. Harnessing the potential of these hidden leaders is paramount to fostering an environment where every individual embodies the spirit of ownership and leadership.

Recognizing these leaders is the first step. They are the ones who step up when challenges arise, who consistently exhibit a commitment beyond their designated roles, and who inspire others through their actions. But how does one identify such individuals amidst the vast sea of employees?

Titles are mere labels. Leadership and ownership are exhibited through actions, commitment, and influence. Therefore, when seeking out hidden leaders, look for those who take initiative, provide solutions, and have a positive impact on their teams. Once these hidden leaders are identified, the next step is to fortify their leadership skills. This can be achieved through tailored training programs, mentorship, and consistent feedback loops. By investing in their development, not only does the organization amplify their potential, but it also sends a powerful message about the value of leadership at every level.

Hidden leaders, when recognized and nurtured, can set the gold standard for desired behaviors within the company. They become the torchbearers of the ownership culture. By spotlighting their achievements and leadership behaviors, organizations can provide clear, relatable examples for other employees to emulate.

Recognition plays a crucial role in reinforcing desired behaviors. By acknowledging and rewarding the efforts of hidden leaders, companies can motivate others to step up and take ownership. This creates a ripple effect, where leadership behaviors become the norm rather than the exception.

Ingrain Ownership into Company Culture

To ensure that the spirit of ownership permeates every layer of the organization, it's essential to integrate it into the company's core values. Regular workshops, discussions, and training sessions emphasizing the importance of ownership can drive home the message. By identifying and nurturing the hidden leaders within an organization, companies can cultivate a rich, ownership-driven culture. These leaders, once unearthed and empowered, can significantly influence their peers, set commendable standards, and lead by example. As they rise and shine, they pave the way for others, transforming what was once hidden into one of the company's most palpable and invaluable assets. In this environment, everyone is not just an employee;

they're leaders in their own right, steering the organization toward collective success.

THE NECESSITY OF HANDS-ON LEADERSHIP: STEERING THE SHIP WITH FORESIGHT

In the intricate ballet of business, leaders often find themselves poised on a tightrope. On one end lies the allure of the grand vision, the bigger picture that promises future successes. On the other end are the daily operations, the minutiae that demand attention and precision. Striking the right balance is the key to not only maintaining stability but also propelling the business forward.

The Visionary's Dilemma...business foresight just happens to change from person to person. We have seen this movie before.

Every groundbreaking enterprise begins with a vision. This vision, a concoction of ambition, foresight, and innovation, charts the course for the business's journey. However, vision alone cannot navigate the tumultuous waters of the business world. It requires a hands-on approach from the leader and a commitment to steering the ship themselves rather than relying solely on the crew, no matter how skilled.

Why is this hands-on approach crucial, especially when a leader already has a competent managerial team in place? Managers are often equipped with a keen sense of the present. They excel at streamlining processes, managing teams, and ensuring that day-to-day operations run smoothly. Their expertise is invaluable. However, their perspective is frequently rooted in the present, molded by immediate challenges and short-term goals.

The business leader, on the other hand, must possess the ability to see beyond the horizon. Their gaze should be set not just on the challenges of today but on the potentialities of tomorrow. Their vision encompasses market shifts, emerging trends, and potential innovations. And herein lies the rub: this vision, so evident to the leader, may not always be discernible to the management team.

Guiding the Course: The Hands-On Imperative

When leaders detach themselves from the daily workings of their business, they risk creating a chasm. This gap between the grand vision and ground reality can inadvertently lead managers to steer the company in directions misaligned with the intended trajectory.

Being hands-on doesn't mean micromanaging or undermining the authority of the managerial team. It means many things. Leaders should be familiar with the inner workings of their company, understand processes, and be available for critical decisions. Sharing the broader vision, market insights, and long-term strategies with the managerial team ensures alignment. It bridges the gap between what is and what could be. By mentoring key personnel, leaders can cultivate a shared vision, ensuring that future decision-makers carry forward the company's foundational principles and aspirations.

Creating systems where feedback flows seamlessly from the ground up allows leaders to gauge if the bigger picture is resonating with every tier of the company. While the importance of a hands-on leadership approach is undeniable, it's equally vital to recognize and value the expertise of the managerial team. They provide the ballast, ensuring that the ship, even as it's guided by the leader's vision, remains steady and doesn't capsize amidst daily challenges.

To truly succeed and bring a vision to fruition, business leaders must immerse themselves in the tapestry of their enterprise. Only by intertwining the threads of foresight with the colors of daily operations can they weave a masterpiece that stands the test of time.

CEO Perspective:

As a CEO, the temptation to adopt a hands-off leadership style can be strong, especially when you're surrounded by a team of competent managers and executives. After all, delegation is a critical skill in leadership. However, there's a fine line between empowering your team and becoming disconnected from the day-to-day realities of your business. In today's fast-moving, unpredictable landscape, hands-on leadership has never been more essential. But let me clarify: being hands-on doesn't mean micromanaging. It's about steering the ship with foresight, about being intricately connected with the various elements that make your organization tick so you can guide it effectively through both calm and turbulent waters.

First, let's talk about the role of foresight. It's an attribute that comes from a deep understanding of your industry, market trends, employee sentiments, and emerging technologies. Foresight enables you to anticipate opportunities and threats, providing you with the valuable lead time needed to prepare and adjust your strategies. As a hands-on leader, I make it a point to keep my ear to the ground, spending time with teams across functions and levels to understand the challenges they face and the tools they need to succeed. This helps me to build a more realistic and robust strategic vision for the company.

In addition to foresight, hands-on leadership means having a nuanced understanding of your managerial team's capabilities and limitations. No one is perfect, and recognizing where the gaps lie allows you to bring in the right resources, training, or even external hires to strengthen the team. The better you understand what's happening on the ground, the more equipped you are to provide the specific guidance and resources your managers need to excel.

Being hands-on also allows for real-time problem-solving and decision-making. In today's digital age, situations evolve at a breakneck speed, and waiting for a quarterly review to address issues is often too late. A hands-on approach enables quick identification of challenges and immediate action. It also provides an avenue for instant feedback for both you and your team, creating a culture of continuous improvement.

Importantly, hands-on leadership is not just about business metrics; it's about people. When you're closely involved, you can gauge the pulse of the organization's morale, making you better equipped to tackle issues like employee engagement, attrition, or team conflicts before they escalate. It humanizes the role of the CEO, breaking down the hierarchical barriers that can often stifle innovation and candid communication.

Lastly, being hands-on sets a powerful example for your management team. It sends a clear message that attentiveness, thoroughness, and deep engagement are valued traits within the organization. Leaders set the cultural tone, and by embodying these qualities, you encourage your managers to adopt a similar approach with their own teams.

To sum it up, hands-on leadership is not an archaic concept but an evolving, adaptive style that's crucial for navigating the complexities of modern business. It brings with it the gifts of foresight, real-time problem-solving, and a more cohesive, engaged workforce. While the helm of the ship may have sophisticated navigational tools, nothing replaces the nuanced judgment and situational awareness of a captain who's truly in touch with every element of their vessel.

ALBERT" BEYOND MONETARY MOTIVATIONS: PROVIDING CLARITY AND DIRECTION

Gorilla Inc. had been riding high on its recent successes, particularly with its ventures into the digital realm. The employee morale was visibly boosted with the various initiatives in play. However, Albert, the ever-observant middle manager, noticed an undercurrent of restlessness among some of his peers and subordinates.

During an informal coffee chat with Clara, a team leader, Albert got a hint of the issue. "Albert," she said, "I appreciate the bonuses and pay hikes. But sometimes, I just feel lost. I wish I knew more about where we're headed, not just how much we'll be paid when we get there."

It was a lightbulb moment for Albert. He realized that while monetary incentives were crucial, they weren't the sole driving force for many at Gorilla Inc. People sought purpose, clarity, and a clear sense of direction.

Determined to address this, Albert conceptualized the "North Star Sessions." These weren't just regular company meetings; they were spaces where the company's vision, mission, and future direction were discussed transparently. More than mere presentations, they were collaborative sessions where leaders shared the big picture, and employees could ask questions, share their concerns, or even provide suggestions.

Albert kickstarted the first session with an insightful presentation, not about quarterly targets but about the company's five-year vision. Where did Gorilla Inc. see itself in the market? What values would they uphold? How would they adapt to industry changes? It was all laid out.

But the real magic happened post-presentation. Employees engaged in spirited discussions, brainstorming sessions, and interactive workshops to align their individual roles with the broader company vision. They left the session not just with a sense of clarity but also a sense of belonging and purpose.

The impact of the "North Star Sessions" was profound. Employees felt more aligned with the company's goals, understanding not just the 'what' but the 'why' of their roles. Productivity soared, but more importantly, job satisfaction rates reached unprecedented levels. It turned out that clarity and direction were as significant, if not more, as the paycheck at the end of the month.

<u>Reflection:</u> In the fast-paced corporate world, it's easy to get caught up in numbers, targets, and financial incentives. But Albert's intervention at Gorilla Inc. underscores a vital lesson: true motivation transcends monetary rewards. For employees to be genuinely engaged and committed, they need to see the bigger picture, understand their role in it, and feel valued beyond their paycheck. By offering clarity, direction, and a sense of purpose, companies can foster a dedicated, passionate, and, most importantly, content workforce.

Chapter 7: Cultivating A Thriving Managerial Ecosystem: Deepening The Roots Of Leadership

While the previous sections of Chapter 7 delved into the multifaceted ecosystem of managerial success, it's imperative to deepen our understanding of how to genuinely embed these principles into everyday managerial operations. By diving into each facet more profoundly, we can equip managers to navigate challenges and lead their teams with unmatched resilience and adaptability.

"Empathy" goes beyond understanding team dynamics. Managers should recognize the individual aspirations, fears, and motivations of each team member. By doing so, they can tailor their leadership style, creating an environment where each member feels valued and understood. Companies like "Salesforce," which consistently ranks high in the best places to work, often emphasize the importance of empathy in their leadership training.

While managers need to collaborate across departments, they should also facilitate such collaborations for their teams. Breaking silos can lead to a cross-pollination of ideas, fostering innovation. "Pixar," for instance, designs its workspace to encourage unplanned interactions, recognizing that these serendipitous moments can lead to groundbreaking ideas.

Managers should develop a macro lens, training themselves to understand global trends and market shifts. But it's not just about awareness. They should be adept at breaking down these macro insights into micro strategies for their teams. Consider how "Lego" rebounded after nearly going bankrupt in the early 2000s. Managers, in tune with digital play trends, diversified the brand into movies, mobile games, and more, transforming its fortunes.

Beyond addressing mental health, organizations should recognize that managerial well-being is holistic, encompassing physical, emotional, social, and spiritual dimensions. Integrating regular physical activity, promoting social interactions outside of work contexts, or even facilitating spiritual or meditative retreats can have profound impacts. Companies like "Nike" have integrated holistic wellness into their culture, offering on-site gyms, mindfulness sessions, and more.

While the growth mindset is vital, nurturing an innate curiosity can make managers more adaptable and innovative. By constantly questioning, seeking answers, and being open to new experiences, managers can remain ahead of the curve. "Google's" famous '20% time' policy, allowing employees to work on passion projects, is a testament to the power of curiosity.

Feedback isn't just about collecting viewpoints; it's also about fostering an environment where differing opinions are encouraged. Managers should be secure enough to welcome dissent and constructive criticism, using these as tools to refine strategies. Companies like "Bridgewater Associates" emphasize "radical transparency," believing that open disagreements, when handled constructively, lead to better decisions.

In essence, embedding the principles of a thriving managerial ecosystem isn't about introducing a set of rules or guidelines. It's about cultivating a mindset and environment that's adaptive, empathetic, curious, and collaborative. As managers deepen their roots in this rich soil of holistic leadership, they become not just effective overseers but transformative leaders capable of guiding their teams through the most challenging terrains.

DEEPENING THE ROOTS OF LEADERSHIP: SEIZING EVERY OPPORTUNITY

In the journey towards becoming a leader, the corner office and the resounding title are merely symbols. True leadership springs from a mindset, a collection of behaviors, and an innate drive to influence and inspire others. This drive is something that can be cultivated long before official recognition comes your way. To deepen the roots of leadership, one must proactively seek out experiences and opportunities that shape and hone leadership skills.

While aspiring for leadership roles in the future, it's imperative to excel in the present. Your current role offers a platform to demonstrate dedication, expertise, and the potential to take on more significant challenges. The pursuit of leadership shouldn't overshadow the responsibilities of today. As Muriel Maignan Wilkins wisely suggests, your performance in your current role is the foundational step towards ascending to leadership positions.

Being a leader doesn't just mean leading teams; it also involves helping other leaders, especially your immediate superiors, achieve their objectives. Demonstrating reliability, taking on crucial projects, and continuously seeking ways to alleviate challenges that your superiors face can position you as a valuable asset. By leaning more towards saying "yes" and offering solutions, you not only cement your reliability but also exemplify leadership traits.

The quest for leadership doesn't confine you to the boundaries of your designated role or even your professional life. It's about adopting an attitude of "I can lead this" in every situation. Be it volunteering for a new company initiative, mediating a challenging situation among peers, or taking on community-based roles – every experience is an opportunity to display leadership qualities. As Watkins highlights, these pursuits, big or small, reflect an individual's aspiration and potential for leadership.

Leadership isn't just about managing teams or taking significant decisions; it's also about being present, participating, and contributing to various aspects of an organization's functioning. From facilitating a meeting, assisting in recruitment drives, or merely stepping in to provide a fresh perspective, leadership opportunities are abundant. And often, the most impactful opportunities are the unexpected ones. Outside the confines of work, community roles, non-profit involvement, or any initiative that brings about positive change can be platforms to showcase leadership.

In essence, leadership isn't a destination; it's a continuous journey. By staying committed to present responsibilities, aiding superiors, and seizing every opportunity to lead, regardless of its scale, aspiring leaders can deepen their leadership roots. The groundwork for becoming a recognized leader is laid much before the recognition itself; it's constructed through consistent actions, a proactive mindset, and an unwavering commitment to growth and excellence.

CEO Perspective

In the digital era, cultivating a thriving managerial ecosystem isn't just a buzzword; it's a necessity for organizational resilience and success. As a CEO, one of my most critical roles is to nourish this delicate web of human interactions, skills, and workflows. This starts by deepening the roots of leadership, transcending the traditional boundaries of hierarchical command to emphasize emotional intelligence, adaptability, and a culture of continuous learning.

But how do we build effective teams in this digital age, with its unique challenges and opportunities? One key aspect is leveraging technology to enhance communication. Remote work and hybrid models have become the norm rather than the exception, making it crucial to integrate technology that fosters seamless communication and collaboration. Yet, technology is merely a tool; the culture of openness, trust, and teamwork breathes life into these digital platforms.

Data-driven decision-making is another cornerstone. In today's connected world, data is readily available, but what matters is how we use it. Managers must be trained not just to collect data but to interpret it, turning raw numbers into actionable insights that can drive strategic business decisions. The manager of today is both an analyst and a strategist, well-versed in the language of data yet equally fluent in the art of human relations.

Additionally, the rapid pace of technological change brings an element of constant flux, requiring adaptability and flexibility that go beyond the typical job description. Teams need to be prepared to pivot, innovate, and adapt to new tools or processes quickly. In this climate, managers must be champions of change, cultivating a team culture where transformation is not just anticipated but welcomed. They become the navigators in our journey through uncharted waters, combining the foresight to see obstacles ahead with the agility to alter course as needed.

In the realm of digital literacy, it's not enough for managers to merely keep up with the latest tools and technologies. The expectation now is for them to be digital leaders, continually acquiring new skills and using them to improve both team performance and business outcomes. Investing in regular training and skills development in this area equips managers not only to cope with change but also to drive it.

Yet, at the core of this managerial ecosystem is synergy—the belief that our collective efforts exceed the sum of individual contributions. Collaboration trumps competition; diverse viewpoints are treasured for the richness they bring, and a sense of shared ownership pervades the organization. It's an ecosystem where every manager is not just responsible for their own department but feels a deep sense of accountability for the company's overall well-being.

So, as the CEO, I see myself as both the gardener, nurturing the growth and health of this intricate ecosystem, and the architect, meticulously designing its structural flow and dynamics. A well-cultivated managerial ecosystem is not merely a mechanism for organizational success; it's the lifeblood that enables the company to adapt, evolve, and thrive in the fast-paced digital landscape.

Leading By Example: An Unwavering Commitment To Excellence

Every company has its ethos, a unique spirit that sets it apart. In the world of business, while structures, strategies, and systems play undeniable roles, it's often the intangible, the passion and dedication of its leaders, that leaves an indelible mark. My journey with our healthcare company offers a testament to this principle.

In an era where CEOs and company founders often find themselves ensconced in boardrooms, I chose a path less trodden. Leadership, in my view, is not just about decision-making from an elevated platform; it's about immersing oneself in the very fabric of the organization.

Why do I believe so? Because a company's heartbeat isn't found in its financial statements or strategic blueprints but in its corridors, meeting rooms, and, yes, even its bathrooms.

My decision to be hands-on, to the extent of coming in on weekends and cleaning the bathrooms, isn't about micromanagement or a lack of trust in my team. It's a statement, a message to every member of our organization that no task is too small and no responsibility insignificant.

Healthcare, after all, is about care in its purest form. It's about tending to those in need, ensuring cleanliness and hygiene, and prioritizing the well-being of our patients above all. If I, as the leader, shirk away from any aspect of this, how can I expect my team to uphold these values with unwavering commitment?

My presence, working harder and showing up more than my managers, is a conscious strategy. Leaders have a unique power—the power to inspire through action. When the team sees me not as an abstract figure but as someone working alongside them, it fosters a culture of collective ownership. It sends a clear message: We're in this together. If I do not read, they won't read. If I do not work, they will not work.

This approach has yielded palpable benefits. The team's morale has surged, there's a tangible sense of camaraderie, and our patient satisfaction metrics have witnessed an uptick. More than the numbers, it's the feedback—both from the staff and our patients—that validates this approach. They see the commitment, the genuine care, and it resonates.

As our healthcare company continues to grow, my vision remains unaltered. While we will undoubtedly scale, innovate, and evolve, the essence—the commitment to excellence and hands-on leadership—will remain our North Star.

Incorporating this ethos into our daily operations is more than just a leadership strategy; it's a reflection of our identity. An identity that says: In a world of ever-changing dynamics, our commitment to care, excellence, and leading by example will remain steadfast.

The Dance of Leadership: Shane, Max, and a Spirited Rivalry

In every organization's journey, there emerge characters that are pivotal, personalities that enliven the narrative with their distinctive shades. In our healthcare company's tale, Shane and Max play such roles, each bringing a dynamic energy that propels our collective spirit.

Shane: The Vigilant Challenger

Shane, our director, is not just any leader. With a hawk's eye for detail and a penchant for perfection, he keeps a close watch on all of us, including me. While it's uncommon for a director to "keep tabs" on the CEO, Shane's approach is anything but conventional. His belief is simple: leadership is not exempt from scrutiny or growth.

In many ways, Shane's relentless drive to challenge me has turned our professional rapport into a friendly competition. Each day poses a new challenge, a new opportunity to outdo the other. While some might perceive this as a mere rivalry, for us, it's a symbiotic dance. Shane's challenges aren't criticisms but invigorating jolts that keep me on my toes. His "tabs" are not surveillance but reminders of our shared commitment to excellence.

Max's Induction into the Fold

Then there's Max. Young, spirited, and bursting with innovative ideas, Max could have easily been overwhelmed by our company's energetic pace and the intense dynamic between Shane and me. But Shane, with his unique leadership style, ensured that Max became an integral part of this rhythm.

Drawing from our competitive camaraderie, Shane began channeling the same energy towards mentoring Max. By setting challenges, keeping a close eye on his progress, and sometimes indulging in friendly bouts of competition, Shane was doing for Max what he did for me – igniting the fire of relentless pursuit.

Max, with his inherent zeal, embraced this dynamic wholeheartedly. The challenges posed by Shane became milestones for him to surpass. Each feedback, each piece of advice became stepping stones to his personal and professional growth.

A Triad of Growth and Motivation

The interplay between Shane, Max, and me has transformed our healthcare company's leadership dynamics. It's no longer just about individual roles or hierarchies. It's about collective growth, shared aspirations, and a mutual respect that transcends titles.

This spirited rivalry, underpinned by deep trust and mutual respect, has yielded tangible benefits for our company. It has fostered an environment where complacency has no place. Instead, there's a continual strive for betterment, a ceaseless quest for excellence. As our narrative unfolds, it becomes clear that what Shane initiated isn't merely a competition. It's a legacy. A legacy of striving, challenging, and uplifting each other. Through this dynamic, we're not just building a successful healthcare company; we're sculpting a culture. A culture where every individual, from the CEO to the newest recruit, is continually inspired to be the best version of themselves.

Channeling Energy: Igniting Middle Management Through Spirited Leadership

The soul of a company isn't determined merely by its top-tier executives or its frontline workers. Instead, it lies in the cohesive effort of every tier, every individual. Often, middle management becomes the linchpin, bridging the strategic vision of top leadership with the operational reality of ground-level teams. Yet, ensuring this vital group is engaged, motivated, and invested in the company's success can be challenging. Our story, rich with the dynamics between Shane, Max, and me, offers insights into how an energized leadership team can inspire middle management to care deeply about company success.

Energy and enthusiasm are contagious. When leadership is vibrant, passionate, and fully invested, it sets a precedent that's hard to ignore. Shane's relentless drive, Max's infectious zeal, and my hands-on commitment created an ecosystem of fervor and dedication. This environment, marked by spirited rivalry and mutual respect, became the standard, not the exception.

Middle managers, often caught between strategic decisions and ground realities, found themselves enveloped in this energy. They bore witness to a leadership team that wasn't content with mere directives but was engaged in the trenches alongside them.

Our leadership dynamics transcended traditional hierarchies. It wasn't about the CEO, the director, or the rising star; it was about a shared purpose, collective growth, and mutual challenges. This flattened perception of power dynamics made middle management feel more connected, seeing leadership not as distant decision-makers but as hands-on allies.

When leaders lead by example, it promotes a sense of ownership. Middle managers, influenced by our dedication, began viewing the company's success not as a directive from the top but as a personal mission. The company's victories became their victories, its challenges their challenges.

The mentorship dynamic between Shane and Max highlighted an essential aspect of professional growth—continuous learning and challenges. This served as a model for middle managers, emphasizing the significance of mentorship and continuous evolution.

Recognizing this, many middle managers sought mentors within the organization, aiming to emulate the growth trajectory they saw in Max. Additionally, they began mentoring their own teams, creating a cascading effect of knowledge sharing and skill enhancement.

Our leadership team's approach to feedback, marked by mutual respect and the intent to uplift, showcased the importance of open dialogue. Middle managers, inspired by this, fostered open channels of communication with their teams. This not only helped in identifying operational bottlenecks but also ensured that every team member felt valued and heard.

In the intricate symphony of corporate success, middle management plays a critical role, harmonizing the grand visions with ground realities. Our leadership team, through its passion, dedication, and mutual challenges, set the tempo. This rhythm resonated deeply with middle managers, transforming them from mere executors of strategy to invested stakeholders, deeply caring about the company's success. The result? A cohesive force, unified in vision and purpose, propelling the company towards unparalleled achievements.

"Albert" Cultivating A Thriving Managerial Ecosystem: Deepening the Roots of Leadership

It had been a series of transformative months for Gorilla Inc., with initiatives breathing life and direction into its corporate culture. The onus of these changes, Albert realized, lay not just with the top-tier leadership but also with managers like him, often termed the "middle layer." This layer was crucial – acting as the conduit between overarching corporate strategies and the grassroots level execution. However, in many corporations, middle management is often the most overlooked, leading to a disconnected ecosystem.

Albert's experiences had taught him that for a company to be agile, innovative, and adaptive, its managerial layer needed to be robust, connected, and deeply rooted in the company's ethos.

With this in mind, Albert proposed the "Deep Roots Initiative." This initiative aimed to strengthen the managerial layer by focusing on the following essential pillars:

In the ever-evolving business world, managers couldn't afford to stagnate. The initiative introduced regular workshops, courses, and training sessions tailored for managers, focusing not just on technical skills but also on leadership, strategic thinking, and industry trends.

Recognizing that the best learning often happens through shared experiences, Albert introduced bi-monthly managerial meetups. These weren't formal meetings but relaxed gatherings where managers could discuss challenges, share insights, and learn from one another.

To ensure the managerial layer felt heard and valued, Albert established dedicated feedback channels. Managers could provide feedback about strategies, initiatives, or any challenges they faced. This feedback was then reviewed at the top tier, ensuring that valuable on-ground insights didn't get lost.

As months rolled into years, the impact of the "Deep Roots Initiative" became palpable. The managers at Gorilla Inc. were more informed, connected, and empowered. They didn't just execute strategies; they contributed to shaping them. Their teams noticed the difference too, benefitting from more competent, confident, and connected leadership.

Albert would often say, "A tree is only as strong as its roots." And true to his words, by strengthening its managerial roots, Gorilla Inc. didn't just survive; it thrived, branching out into new avenues and reaching unprecedented heights.

<u>Reflection:</u> A company's leadership isn't just about its top-tier executives. The middle managers play an equally pivotal role in shaping its destiny. By investing in their growth, networking, and empowerment, companies can build a solid foundation, ensuring stability, innovation, and growth. Albert's journey in this chapter underscores the importance of deepening the roots of leadership, cultivating an ecosystem where managers don't just follow but lead, inspire, and thrive.

Chapter 8: The Legacy of Leadership: Crafting a Managerial Blueprint for the Future

The legacy of a manager extends beyond their immediate tenure. Great managers influence the trajectories of their teams, the direction of the organization, and even the broader industry landscape. To secure such a lasting impact, it's imperative for managers to be forward-thinkers and craft a leadership blueprint tailored for tomorrow. Here's how they can do that.

Foresight In Technological Evolution

As technology continues to shape industries, managers must stay a step ahead. Understanding not just current tech tools but also emerging trends can set apart visionary managers from their peers. Organizations like "Apple" have consistently demonstrated the power of foresight, transitioning smoothly from computers to music players, smartphones, and wearables.

Actionable Insight

Managers should regularly participate in tech conferences, subscribe to relevant industry journals, and even consider basic coding courses to grasp the language of tech.

The importance of sustainability is growing exponentially. Managers need to ensure their decisions are economically viable, socially responsible, and environmentally friendly. "Unilever's"

Sustainable Living Plan, which integrates sustainability into the core business strategy, exemplifies this approach.

Managers can begin with a sustainability audit of their department, identifying areas for greener practices or socially beneficial initiatives.

A diverse team offers a wealth of perspectives, fostering creativity and reducing biases. Managers of the future need to champion diversity in all its forms. "Accenture's" commitment to having a gender-balanced workforce by 2025 is a noteworthy initiative in this direction.

Managers should actively participate in unconscious bias training and ensure that recruitment processes prioritize diversity. The half-life of skills is decreasing rapidly. To remain relevant, managers must adopt a student's mindset throughout their careers. Companies like "Siemens" have recognized this, offering continuous learning opportunities for their employees.

Actionable Insight:

Managers should earmark a set number of hours each month for personal development, exploring online courses, seminars, or workshops. While hard skills will continue evolving, EI remains a timeless asset for managers. Understanding, empathizing, and effectively interacting with others can significantly influence a manager's legacy. "Google's" "Project Aristotle" highlighted the importance of soft skills like EI in team success.

Managers should practice active listening, engage in team-building exercises, and even consider counseling sessions to enhance their EI. Legacy is as much about succession as personal achievements. Managers need to identify and nurture future leaders, ensuring a seamless transition and continuity of vision. "Goldman Sachs" has a meticulous grooming process for potential leaders, showcasing the importance of succession planning.

Managers should implement mentorship programs within their departments and offer shadowing opportunities for potential leaders. Crafting a legacy isn't about the fleeting moments of triumph; it's about the enduring impact on individuals, organizations, and industries. As managers pivot towards the future, they must combine foresight with actionable insights, ensuring they leave behind a managerial blueprint that stands the test of time. The future awaits those who are prepared for it, and with the right strategies in place, managers can etch their mark in the annals of leadership excellence.

THE RIPPLE EFFECT OF MANAGERIAL DECISIONS

Every choice made by a manager doesn't merely stop at the decision point; it reverberates throughout the organization, creating a series of ripples. Like a stone tossed into a pond, the initial impact might seem small, but the ensuing waves touch every part of the organization, influencing people, processes, and profits.

Effective communication isn't just about transferring information; it's about inspiring, motivating, and clarifying. Managers play a pivotal role in ensuring that messages are not just delivered but are understood, internalized, and acted upon. Companies, where communication thrives, witness fewer mistakes, reduced rework, and better alignment toward organizational goals. Effective communication ensures everyone is rowing in the same direction, maximizing efficiency and cohesion.

Trust isn't a luxury; it's a necessity. Managers who trust their teams foster an environment where risks are taken, creativity flourishes, and individuals feel a sense of ownership. This empowerment breeds responsibility, accountability, and a drive to succeed. When employees feel trusted and empowered, they're more likely to go the extra mile, take initiative, and feel a deeper connection to the company's success. This not only boosts productivity but also leads to greater job satisfaction and retention. Managers need to understand that feedback isn't a one-way street. While providing constructive feedback to team members is essential, managers must also be open to receiving feedback about their decisions, leadership style, and the overall health of the organization. Organizations that have established healthy feedback loops are more agile. They can pivot quickly, rectify mistakes before they become costly, and adapt to the changing needs of their workforce and market. In an age defined by rapid changes, agility is more than a buzzword; it's a survival trait. Managers should be leading the charge, promoting flexibility in strategies, adaptability in teams, and a willingness to change course when necessary.

Relevance to Company Success

An agile organization can respond to market shifts, capitalize on emerging opportunities, and mitigate unforeseen risks faster than its competitors. This agility can be a significant differentiator in a volatile market. Modern managers recognize that employee well-being isn't just about attractive perks or health benefits. It's about mental health, work-life balance, recognition, and creating a nurturing work environment.

Relevance to Company Success: When employees feel genuinely cared for, they become the organization's biggest ambassadors. Their increased morale and well-being often translate into improved productivity, reduced absenteeism, and a stronger employer brand.

As we delve deeper into the myriad roles and responsibilities of a manager, it becomes clear that their influence is both profound and pervasive. A manager's decisions, strategies, and leadership approach set the tone for the company's culture, operational efficiency, and future trajectory. While the challenges are manifold, the rewards of effective management—both for the individual manager and for the organization at large—are immense. It's a journey of continuous learning, adaptability, and a relentless pursuit of excellence. In this crucible of challenges and opportunities, the legends of tomorrow's corporate world will be forged.

Crafting a Blueprint for Individual Success - Bridging Ambition and Achievement

Success in leadership is a multidimensional endeavor that goes beyond merely accomplishing tasks. It's about identifying opportunities, establishing relationships, and positioning oneself as a valuable contributor to the organization. Crafting a blueprint for success involves a blend of proactive initiatives, strategic relationship-building, and maintaining an authentic presence. Here's how you can bridge your ambition and achievements to emerge as a successful leader.

In every organization, there are unmet needs, untapped potential, or unnoticed issues - these represent the "white space." Seizing these opportunities sets you apart and showcases your initiative and problem-solving skills. Whether it's addressing an unmet customer need, proposing cost-saving measures, or tackling overlooked problems, filling the white space demonstrates your proactive approach and commitment to the organization's success.

Sharing your aspirations with your manager can be beneficial, provided it's done with a focus on the organization's best interests. When discussing your ambitions, frame them in terms of your contributions to the company. Engage in two-way conversations with your boss, focusing on the bigger picture rather than solely on your aspirations. If your manager may feel threatened by your ambitions, it's better to let your actions speak for your potential.

Identify individuals who have successfully reached positions you aspire to and observe their actions, communication, and demeanor. Seek opportunities to work with them, perhaps by volunteering for their committees or assisting in their projects. Emulate their behaviors that resonate with you, ensuring you stay authentic and not merely imitate them. Moreover, learn from those who seem stuck in their careers, observing what behaviors hinder their progress.

The saying goes, "It's not who you know, it's who knows you." When being considered for a promotion, having supporters across the organization is essential. Cultivate relationships with colleagues and superiors, ensuring that they are aware of your contributions. Every interaction, even seemingly informal ones, is an opportunity to demonstrate your value and knowledge of the business. Be prepared to share your achievements and initiatives when asked.

While ambition is essential for progress, it's crucial to balance it with humility and respect. Avoid overstepping boundaries or trying to exert authority where it's not warranted. Embrace "steward leadership," focusing on the team's goals instead of solely your own. Display "humble confidence" by showcasing appropriate modesty in your role while exuding self-assurance in your ability to rise to higher levels.

The blueprint for success in leadership involves a well-rounded approach, combining proactive initiatives, strategic relationship-building, and authentic interactions. By filling the white space, tactfully sharing your ambitions, finding role models, building relationships, and staying humble and respectful, you can effectively bridge your ambition and achievements, crafting a path to successful leadership.

PART 2: THE INNER LADDER: WEIGHING THE PROS AND CONS OF PROMOTING FROM WITHIN A CEO'S PERSPECTIVE

Promoting from within is a strategy that can inspire a lot of confidence within your organization, but it's not without its risks. When you elevate an employee to a managerial position, you're making a strong statement about your company's culture and values. However, internal promotions can also lead to various challenges that require careful consideration. Here's my take on why promoting from within can be both good and bad.

The Good

Fostering Loyalty and Reducing Turnover

Promoting from within shows that you value loyalty and career development, which can, in turn, lead to a more committed workforce and reduced turnover. People are more likely to stay with a company where they see a clear career path ahead.

Speed of Onboarding

Internal candidates already understand the company culture, systems, and team dynamics. This can dramatically reduce the onboarding time needed for them to be effective in their new managerial roles, allowing for a smoother transition and quicker returns.

Enhancing Employee Morale

Seeing a colleague ascend the ranks can be a powerful motivator for other employees. It sends a message that hard work and dedication are rewarded, thereby boosting overall morale and encouraging a culture of high performance.

Cost-Effectiveness

It's often more cost-effective to promote from within than to recruit externally. The costs associated with external recruitment—including advertising, interviews, and training—can add up quickly.

Cultivating a Cohesive Culture

Internal promotions help maintain a consistent and cohesive company culture. Externally recruited managers can sometimes bring in different values or practices that may not align easily with your existing culture, requiring further adjustments.

The Bad

Promoting exclusively from within can limit the diversity of thought and experience within your leadership team. This lack of external perspectives can be a significant drawback in today's rapidly changing business environment, where innovation and adaptability are key.

Potential for Favoritism

Internal promotions can sometimes lead to claims of favoritism, which can be corrosive to team morale. Such perceptions can lead to a toxic work environment where politics overshadow performance. An excellent individual contributor may not necessarily make an excellent manager. The skill sets required for both roles can be drastically different, and not all high-performing employees have the leadership skills necessary for a managerial role.

Promoting an internal candidate might lead to resentment among peers who were also vying for the role. This can result in decreased productivity and morale, as well as potential disruptions to team dynamics. For the employee promoted, managing former peers can be a difficult transition fraught with emotional and relational complexities. It requires finesse and strong interpersonal skills, which not everyone may possess.

Promoting from within is a double-edged sword. It has the potential to enhance loyalty, boost morale, and provide quick returns, but it can also lead to limited perspectives, potential favoritism, and skill gaps that might hurt the team in the long run. As a CEO, it's essential to weigh these factors carefully and consider whether the potential benefits outweigh the risks for each specific managerial vacancy. Often, a balanced approach—

incorporating both internal promotions and external hires depending on the specific needs and circumstances—is the most prudent strategy for building a robust leadership team.

CEO Perspective

As a CEO, I am ever conscious that leadership is not just about achieving quarterly targets or even setting a long-term strategic vision; it's about leaving a legacy. And legacies are not confined to the hallowed halls of the executive suite; they permeate every layer of the organization. This is why I prioritize crafting a managerial blueprint for the future, a living document of sorts that serves as a roadmap for developing leadership at every level—from middle management to their staff.

In the business world, legacy is often thought of in terms of numbers—profit margins, market share, or valuation. While these are undoubtedly important, they are ultimately transient, subject to the vagaries of markets, competition, and innovation. What endures is the culture, the collective mindset, and the skills and leadership acumen we instill in our people. That's the legacy that matters most, and it's one that can sustain the organization through cycles of change, challenges, and opportunities.

So, what does this managerial blueprint look like? At its core, it's a comprehensive leadership development strategy that seeks to identify high-potential talent early and invests in their growth systematically. This isn't about sending people to a week-long workshop and checking a box; it's about integrating leadership development into the very fabric of our daily operations. We leverage real-world projects, mentorship programs, and even cross-functional assignments as live training grounds for budding leaders.

The blueprint also factors in the evolving dynamics of the digital age. It encompasses not just technical skills but also softer skills like emotional intelligence, adaptability, and resilience that are often more challenging to teach but are indispensable in today's complex, fast-paced environment. In essence, it's about creating leaders who are not just digitally proficient but are also human-centric, recognizing that the intersection of technology and humanity is where true innovation lies.

Another critical aspect of this blueprint is the concept of 'leading from every chair.' In the future, leadership won't just be the domain of those with a managerial title; it will need to be a trait exhibited at all levels of the organization. Encouraging this broad-based leadership creates a culture of empowerment and accountability, where each individual feels responsible for the success of the team and the larger organization.

And let's not forget that a blueprint is a dynamic, evolving document. It's not something you create and then file away. It needs to be revisited, reviewed, and revised regularly to ensure that it aligns with the shifting realities of the business landscape. Just like any strategic plan, it requires monitoring, feedback, and periodic updates to remain relevant and effective.

Ultimately, the legacy of leadership I aim to create as CEO is one of enduring strength and adaptability. By focusing on crafting a comprehensive, future-oriented managerial blueprint, I hope to leave behind an organization that doesn't just react to change but anticipates and thrives on it. I want to see a succession of leaders who can carry the torch forward, navigating new challenges with the wisdom, skills, and cultural ethos that we have collectively nurtured. In that lies the true measure of our leadership legacy, one that benefits not just the current generation of leaders and staff but the many that will follow.

Synergy in Motion: Age, Vision, and the Spirit of Commitment

In the corporate maze, it's not uncommon to find companies where individuals work in silos, each ticking off their list of tasks without a genuine connection to the broader vision. But when you step into our company, a different story unfolds. Here, the soul of the company pulsates with the shared heartbeat of every individual, from the CTO to the freshest recruit. A narrative that's particularly brought to life by Thomas, Billy, Tom, and myself.

Thomas: Defying Age with Unyielding Spirit

Age is often seen as a harbinger of slowing down, a time to step back and let the younger generation take the reins. But when you meet our CTO, Thomas, any such preconceived notions are promptly dispelled. At 60, Thomas isn't just keeping pace; he's setting it. His vigor, unmatched even by those half his age, is rooted in a deep-seated feeling of ownership.

Thomas doesn't view the company as just another job or a twilight stint before retirement. He sees himself as an integral part of its present and future. This sense of belonging, of being woven into the very fabric of the organization, fuels his drive. It's not about individual achievements for Thomas; it's about ensuring the collective success of the company he has grown to love and cherish.

Our office is more than just a physical space. It's a crucible where ideas meld, challenges are tackled, and visions are forged.

This becomes most evident when Billy, Tom, and I converge. While each of us brings unique perspectives and skills to the table, our alignment in thought and purpose is uncanny.

When the three of us work together, it's not a mere juxtaposition of roles. It's a symphony. Whether it's charting out strategies, addressing operational challenges, or envisioning the future, our discussions are marked by a shared understanding of company goals. This unity in purpose ensures that not only are things getting done but that they're getting done right. What sets our company apart is the pervasive sense of collective ownership. This sentiment isn't confined to the top echelons but permeates every layer. Whether it's Thomas, with his indomitable spirit and commitment, or the collaborative trio of Billy, Tom, and myself, there's a shared understanding: The company's success is personal.

This ethos ensures that tasks aren't merely ticked off a checklist. They are pursued with passion and an understanding of the larger impact. Every decision, every action is weighed against the backdrop of the company's overarching vision. Every company has its stories, its legends. In our narrative, it's the tales of people like Thomas, who defy conventions and age, driven by sheer passion. It's about the synergy of minds like Billy, Tom, and myself, who, despite our distinct roles, are bound by a shared vision.

As we pen the chapters of our company's journey, it's clear that our strength lies not just in our strategies or innovations but in our people. It's in the spirit of commitment, the alignment of purpose, and the unyielding drive to see our shared vision come to fruition. Through this unified effort, we're not just building a company; we're crafting a legacy, while having a great time as a team.

Now let's see what Albert is up to and how he incorporates this:

"Albert" Crafting the Managerial Blueprint: Albert's Vision for the Future

The Gorilla Inc. headquarters was abuzz with excitement. It wasn't just any day; it was the day Albert was slated to present his comprehensive managerial vision, a culmination of his years of observations, experiments, and insights. A day that would potentially reshape the managerial dynamics of Gorilla Inc. for the years to come.

Albert stood confidently, his slides depicting not just data points but stories, reflections, and journeys. The narrative he weaved wasn't about micro-management or an exhaustive rulebook. Instead, it was about creating a blueprint, a flexible framework that would allow managers to innovate while staying aligned with the company's overarching goals.

His Blueprint Centered Around Four Core Tenets

1. Empowerment Over Control: Albert stressed the importance of empowering managers with decision-making authority. By entrusting them with responsibilities and ensuring they had the requisite resources, the company could foster a culture of ownership and proactive problem-solving.

2. Continuous Evolution The business world is not static, and neither should be the approach to management. Albert emphasized the importance of continuous learning, advocating for periodic training, upskilling, and exposure to industry trends.

3. Holistic Well-being: Recognizing that a manager's effectiveness isn't just about professional acumen, Albert highlighted the importance of mental, emotional, and physical well-being. Initiatives promoting work-life balance, mental health awareness, and physical fitness were integral to his blueprint.

4. Open Dialogue Channels: Communication, Albert believed, was the lifeblood of effective management. He advocated for the creation of platforms where managers could freely communicate with top leadership, share feedback, voice concerns, and even brainstorm innovative solutions.

Albert concluded his presentation with a poignant statement: "The future of Gorilla Inc. doesn't lie in machines, algorithms, or even market trends. It lies in its people, especially those who lead, guide, and inspire others. Let's equip them, empower them, and elevate them. The rest will follow."

The applause that followed was not just in appreciation of a well-crafted blueprint but in acknowledgment of a vision that resonated with everyone present.

Reflection: Leadership isn't about casting a shadow of control but about illuminating the path for others. Albert's journey through Gorilla Inc. showcases the evolution of managerial roles, emphasizing adaptability, empathy, and empowerment. His final blueprint isn't just a roadmap for Gorilla Inc. but a testament to the pivotal role managers play in shaping a company's destiny. Through foresight, innovation, and a people-first approach, managers can usher in an era of sustainable growth, collaboration, and excellence.

Albert's Odyssey: A Tapestry of Lessons, Insights, and Horizons

The sun painted a golden hue on the city skyline as Albert sat in his office at Gorilla Inc., gazing out at the vast expanse. His room was adorned not just with accolades and awards but with mementos, each narrating a chapter of his journey.

He took a moment to reflect on his odyssey - from the greenhorn manager eager to make a mark to the visionary leader who had charted a transformative course for Gorilla Inc. Each challenge, each triumph, each setback, and every leap was a thread woven into the rich tapestry of his managerial career.

There was the early phase, filled with enthusiasm yet riddled with rookie mistakes. Albert smiled as he recalled his initial attempts to fit into the corporate mold, only to realize that true leadership lay in authenticity, not conformity.

Then came the challenges - navigating the intricate labyrinths of office politics, deciphering the rapidly evolving technological landscape, and bridging the often yawning gap between top-tier directives and ground-level realities. Yet, with each hurdle, Albert learned, adapted, and emerged stronger, championing initiatives that placed people at the heart of every strategy.

But it wasn't just about the corporate milestones. It was about the relationships he had fostered, the teams he had mentored, and the countless coffee conversations that often sparked the most groundbreaking ideas. Albert realized that while strategies might be crafted in boardrooms, real change was often ignited in hallways, break rooms, and casual chats.

As dusk approached, Albert opened a drawer, pulling out a notebook. It wasn't a corporate ledger or a strategic playbook but a journal filled with scribbles, doodles, and notes. This was Albert's personal chronicle, capturing insights, lessons, and reflections from his journey.

He penned down a note, "Leadership is not a destination but a journey. It's not about reaching a pinnacle but about elevating others as you ascend. It's not about legacy in stone but imprints on souls."

As Albert closed his journal, he felt a sense of contentment. His journey at Gorilla Inc. was not just a professional odyssey but a personal evolution. And while the chapters were many, the essence was singular - leadership, at its core, was about humanity, connection, and endless horizons.

Reflection: Albert's journey at Gorilla Inc. offers a profound lesson for every professional. Beyond strategies, KPIs, and corporate jargon, the essence of leadership is profoundly human. It's about connections, growth, and the infinite potential that lies within every individual. As Albert's odyssey beautifully showcases, the journey is the destination, filled with lessons, memories, and endless horizons.

Now, after all of this information, how do we become more effective?

The Role of Managers in Navigating Employee Development in the Remote Era

The waves of the Great Resignation have sent a clear message to companies worldwide: adapt or lose valuable talent. As employees reassess their career trajectories and priorities, companies find themselves at a pivotal juncture. Employee development, long considered a perk, is now a non-negotiable in talent retention. Managers, with their pivotal role in daily operations and team dynamics, stand front and center in this transformation.

Remote work, while offering flexibility, has thrown a wrench into traditional Learning & Development (L&D) efforts. The challenge is twofold: How do you provide training remotely, and more crucially, how do you ensure engagement?

Enter technology. From cohort-based courses, which foster a sense of community and shared learning, to immersive experiences like virtual reality, companies are innovating fast. Yet, technology alone cannot bridge the gap. The human element, particularly the influence of managers, is irreplaceable.

Managers: The L&D Champions

A Gallup survey I read (Gallup organizational research indicates that at least 70% of the variance in team engagement is explained by the quality of the manager or team leader.) underscores a fundamental truth: managers are the linchpin of team engagement. They have the power to shape, influence, and bolster an employee's experience. So, how can managers help companies become more effective and drive development in this remote age?

1. Personalize Learning Paths: Every individual has unique strengths, weaknesses, and career aspirations. Managers, understanding their team members at a granular level, can tailor training modules to align with personal goals and business objectives.

2. Foster a Culture of Continuous Learning: Managers can inculcate a learning mindset, emphasizing that development is an ongoing journey, not a destination. By setting aside dedicated time for learning or initiating team discussions post-training, they can underscore its importance.

3. Provide Feedback and Recognition: Active feedback after training sessions can reinforce learning. Recognizing and rewarding those who actively participate and apply their learning can also boost morale and motivation.

4. Collaborate with L&D Teams: Instead of viewing the L&D function with skepticism, managers should collaborate closely with them. By providing real-time feedback about team needs and training effectiveness, managers can help shape more impactful programs.

5. Lead by Example: Managers should actively participate in training programs, showcasing their commitment to personal growth and setting a precedent for the team.

6. Facilitate Peer Learning: Encourage team members to share their insights and learnings with each other. Peer-to-peer learning can be incredibly effective, especially when fostered in a supportive environment.

In the ever-evolving landscape of work, particularly in the aftermath of the Great Resignation, managers are not just leaders; they are enablers of growth. By actively championing and adapting L&D efforts in the remote workspace, they can play an instrumental role in attracting, retaining, and nurturing talent. In doing so, they don't just aid individual careers but drive forward the very growth and effectiveness of the companies they serve.

The traditional hierarchy of corporations often places a buffer between the decision-making echelons and those in the trenches. However, when it comes to training and development, those in the trenches - the managers - often have a clearer view of what's needed, what's working, and what's not. To genuinely enhance the skills of a team and foster a culture of continuous learning, it's crucial to tap into this direct source of insights.

It's not hard to see why managers are more attuned to the exact developmental needs of their teams. Day in and day out, they witness the challenges their team members face, understand the gaps in their skill sets, and recognize the potential waiting to be unlocked. It's a vantage point that offers both a detailed view of individual team members and a broader perspective on the team's collective capabilities.

By listening to managers, organizations can ensure that training programs are not just well-intentioned but effectively aligned with real-world requirements. Such alignment increases the likelihood of the training being applied in day-to-day operations, leading to tangible improvements in performance.

It's one thing to acknowledge the importance of managerial feedback and quite another to systematically gather and act on it. Establishing a robust feedback mechanism starts with creating open channels of communication. A regular survey can serve as the bedrock of this system, ensuring that feedback collection is systematic and covers all managers across the organization.

However, the depth and nuances of feedback often emerge in discussions. By setting up forums or focus groups comprising a diverse set of managers, organizations can dive deeper into the feedback. These forums serve a dual purpose. They provide a space for managers to voice their insights and concerns while also allowing the training and development teams to clarify the intent behind certain programs, gather suggestions for improvement, and gauge the reception of new training initiatives.

With a continuous stream of feedback, training initiatives should be viewed as dynamic, evolving entities. As feedback flows in, training programs can be adjusted, refined, or even overhauled to better serve their purpose. This iterative design ensures that training remains relevant, effective, and in tune with the changing needs of teams.

Furthermore, involving managers in the design and review process fosters a sense of ownership. When managers see their feedback leading to tangible changes in training programs, it enhances their buy-in. This increased engagement from managers trickles down to their teams, leading to higher participation and enthusiasm around training initiatives.

In the realm of employee training and development, the voice of the manager is a powerful tool. By tuning into this voice, organizations can craft training initiatives that truly resonate, driving not just skill enhancement but also fostering a culture where continuous learning becomes second nature. After all, in the rapidly evolving business landscape, the ability to learn, adapt, and grow is the ultimate competitive advantage.

CEO Perspective:

In the age of remote work, managers bear a particularly crucial responsibility when it comes to employee development. As a CEO, I've seen firsthand how the dynamics of the workplace have shifted dramatically, transforming the way we think about work, collaboration, and skill development. In this new landscape, managers serve as pivotal touchpoints for their teams, providing direction, structure, and opportunities for growth, even when miles and time zones are apart.

Remote work brings about unique challenges that aren't typically present in a traditional office setting. The absence of physical proximity means managers must go above and beyond to be attuned to their employees' needs and aspirations. The informal opportunities for coaching and mentorship that naturally arise in a physical workspace—those impromptu chats by the coffee machine or quick catch-ups in the hallway—are not readily available in a remote setting. Hence, managers must be proactive in creating spaces for meaningful engagement and feedback, be it through regular one-on-one meetings, virtual coffee chats, or other creative avenues that technology enables.

Employee development in the remote era also demands a rethinking of skillsets. While technical competencies remain critical, soft skills such as self-discipline, effective communication, and time management become even more vital when employees are working independently from diverse locations. Managers should thus tailor their development programs to address these nuanced requirements, perhaps incorporating workshops on remote collaboration tools or setting up peer accountability groups to foster a culture of shared responsibility and growth.

Another area where managers play a critical role is in creating opportunities for real-world application of skills. In a remote environment, the line between training and execution can often blur, given that employees don't have the same ease of access to mentors and colleagues for quick, real-time feedback. Managers must take it upon themselves to build bridges between theoretical learning and practical application, possibly by assigning project roles that stretch employees' current capabilities or by setting up virtual 'hackathons' that encourage innovation and teamwork.

Inclusion is another concern that can't be ignored. The physical distance can sometimes translate into emotional distance, with some team members potentially feeling left out or less engaged. Managers should continually assess the inclusiveness of their remote teams, making sure that development opportunities are equally accessible to everyone, irrespective of their location or working hours. This might mean recording training sessions for those in different time zones or creating mentorship programs that pair employees from diverse backgrounds.

But perhaps most crucially, managers in the remote era need to keep the 'human' in human resources. Working remotely can sometimes lead to feelings of isolation, burnout, or even disconnection from the company culture. Managers should be vigilant about these potential pitfalls, providing emotional support and resources for well-being as a standard part of employee development. After all, a well-rounded, happy employee is often a more productive, engaged one.

So, from my vantage point as CEO, I see the role of managers in navigating employee development in the remote era as multi-dimensional and ever-evolving. It requires a combination of traditional managerial skills, an adaptable mindset, and a deep understanding of the unique challenges and opportunities that remote work presents. As we continue to adapt to this new normal, it's the managers who can seamlessly blend these elements who will be most effective in developing their teams and, by extension, contributing to the long-term success of the organization.

REDEFINING MANAGERIAL TRAINING: A PARADIGM SHIFT FOR THE 21ST CENTURY WORKFORCE

The training of managers often brings to mind images of strategy workshops, performance metrics, and leadership exercises. However, as businesses progress and adapt to the needs of a modern workforce, a fresh approach emerges – one that aligns closer to how students are nurtured in schools. This approach focuses on cognitive growth, showing genuine concern, and setting clear standards of work. By adopting such an educational framework, we can cultivate managers who treat businesses with the same care, dedication, and responsibility they would if the enterprise were their own.

The Power of Cognitive Growth in Leadership

Much like schools instill critical thinking, problem-solving, and creativity in students, the same cognitive nurturing must be extended to our managers. When managers are equipped to think critically and creatively, they can not only address challenges more effectively but also innovate, foresee potential issues, and strategize for long-term success. Moreover, fostering a growth mindset encourages a continuous thirst for learning and improvement, mirroring the ever-evolving landscape of modern businesses.

Nurturing Through Genuine Concern

At the core of any successful educational journey is the relationship between the teacher and the student, built on genuine concern and mutual respect. Similarly, managers, akin to teachers, play a pivotal role in determining the experience of their team members.

Team leaders are positioned uniquely to recognize the strengths of their employees. With 19 million individuals now aware of their strengths, the role of the manager becomes even more critical. By showing genuine concern for their team members, managers can ensure that these individuals leverage their strengths optimally. Recognition for good work, timely feedback, and understanding individual challenges are crucial components of this nurturing process. Such concern not only boosts morale but also fosters a sense of belonging, driving employees to give their best.

Setting Standards Through Clear Work Ethics

Just as educational institutions have curriculums and defined standards of excellence, businesses too, need their own set of clear work standards. When managers have a defined set of standards and ethics, it offers a clear roadmap for decision-making, performance evaluation, and goal-setting. This clarity ensures that managers lead their teams with consistency, fairness, and a vision that aligns with the organization's broader goals.

Furthermore, when standards are clear and consistently upheld, it instills a sense of pride and responsibility in managers. This feeling translates into a deeper connection with the business, treating it with the dedication and care of an owner.

The 21st Century Manager: A Coach for the Modern Workforce

With the workforce's growing awareness of their strengths and aspirations for personalized coaching, the role of the manager is evolving. No longer just a figure of authority, the 21st-century manager is a mentor, a guide, and a coach, closely attuned to the strengths and needs of their team. The rise in engaged workers today is a testament to the shifts taking place in managerial approaches. As workplaces continue to evolve, grounding managerial training in cognitive growth, genuine concern, and clear standards will be paramount to nurturing leaders who inspire, guide, and ultimately lead businesses to new pinnacles of success.

Albert: The Digital Divide: Albert's Quest to Foster Development in the Remote Era

The panoramic view from Albert's office now included a myriad of small digital windows. Gone were the days of bustling office corridors, replaced by the silent pings of instant messages. Gorilla Inc., like many other companies, had adapted to the new normal: remote work.

This shift brought forth a plethora of challenges, and the one weighing heavily on Albert's mind was employee development. Without the tangible interactions of a physical office, how could he ensure that his team not only remained productive but also continued to grow professionally?

The annual "Employee Development Workshop," traditionally an event held at Gorilla Inc.'s conference center, loomed on the calendar. Albert pondered how to translate this into the digital realm without losing its efficacy.

The first step, Albert decided, was to understand the unique challenges the remote setting posed for employee growth. He initiated an anonymous survey among his team, collecting insights about their remote work experience. The responses were eye opening. While many relished the flexibility, they missed the informal learning opportunities - the over-the-shoulder tips, the quick brainstorming sessions at the coffee machine, and the mentorship moments that naturally occurred in an office setting.

Equipped With These Insights, Albert Crafted A Multi-Pronged Approach

Firstly, he introduced the "Digital Mentorship Program." Pairing experienced team members with newer ones, he ensured that the latter received guidance even in a virtual setting. These pairs would have weekly touchpoints, discussing not just immediate work projects but also broader professional development topics.

Secondly, Albert rolled out a series of "Skill Enhancement Webinars." These weren't just the usual corporate presentations but sessions led by team members, showcasing their areas of expertise. This peer-to-peer learning model ensured that knowledge sharing remained robust, even remotely.

Recognizing the importance of informal interactions, Albert initiated "Virtual Coffee Breaks." These were open video calls where team members could join without any specific agenda, replicating the casual chats of an office setting. Surprisingly, these sessions became hotbeds for cross-functional discussions, leading to unexpected collaborations and innovations.

The "Employee Development Workshop" was transformed into a week-long virtual event. It had interactive sessions, break-out groups, and even virtual networking lounges. While it was different from the traditional format, the feedback was overwhelmingly positive, with many finding it more inclusive and accessible.

The true testament to Albert's initiatives' success came during the quarterly review. Not only had productivity remained steady, but there was also a notable improvement in the quality of work, innovative ideas, and collaborative projects. Furthermore, many team members expressed feeling more connected to their peers and more equipped to navigate their professional growth than before.

Reflection: The remote era posed a challenge that Albert turned into an opportunity. Recognizing that the essence of employee development wasn't tied to a physical space but to a mindset of growth, mentorship, and collaboration, Albert showcased that with adaptability and innovation, managers could ensure their teams thrived, irrespective of where they worked. It's a lesson in the timeless nature of genuine leadership and the transient nature of challenges.

The Blueprint of Exceptional Management: Crafting Like-Minded Leadership

In the intricate tapestry of a flourishing organization, one role stands out as the defining thread: the manager. Their influence touches every facet of the business, be it diversity and inclusion, productivity, or even retention. Indeed, their impact is so profound that the manager becomes the heartbeat of an organization, bringing life and energy to every endeavor.

An analysis by Gallup, a renowned name in organizational studies, underscores this significance, revealing that a staggering 70% of the variance in team engagement can be attributed to the quality of management. Such an observation paints a vivid picture - one where the manager, with their actions and decisions, holds the potential to uplift or diminish the spirit and performance of a team.

However, there exists an ironic conundrum. Most managers shape their understanding and practice of management not from structured, evidence-backed training but from the experiences they've had with their past managers. These experiences could be deeply enriching or severely lacking, with the echoes of the past shaping the present. Others base their management style on entrenched stereotypes of leadership, potentially stifling innovation and genuine connection.

To break free from this cycle and foster a breed of like-minded, exceptional managers, businesses must turn to lessons gleaned from the crème de la crème of management across the globe. Here's the distilled wisdom:

The most successful managers bridge the gap between the overarching company purpose and the daily actions of their teams. This alignment creates a cohesive direction, fueling motivation and shared commitment. By actively seeking and valuing the opinions of team members, great managers foster a culture of inclusion and mutual respect. This approach not only garners diverse perspectives but also builds trust and camaraderie. Effective management isn't about sugar-coating feedback or tiptoeing around issues. It's about coaching teams with genuine candor, creating a space where honesty reigns supreme, driving growth and improvement. Committing to a weekly meaningful conversation with each team member ensures that managers stay attuned to their team's challenges, aspirations, and well-being. Each individual has unique drivers and tendencies. By connecting work to these innate motivations, managers can unlock unparalleled enthusiasm and dedication. Recognizing and rewarding outstanding work not only boosts morale but also sets a benchmark for excellence, inspiring others to reach new heights.

An exceptional manager understands that their team members aren't just employees – they're real people with dreams, challenges, and lives outside of work. By caring for them holistically, managers build deeper, more genuine relationships. The mark of a truly great manager is their commitment to developing the next generation of leaders. By making this their foremost responsibility, they ensure the continuous growth and dynamism of the organization.

In essence, the transformative power of a manager cannot be understated. In every challenge and every triumph, their presence is palpable, shaping the destiny of the business. By developing managers who share a like-minded approach to leadership based on the pillars of connection, candor, care, and continuous development, organizations can usher in an era of unparalleled success and engagement.

"Albert" Crafting Like-Minded Leadership: Albert's Tryst with Exceptional Management

The weight of the morning's meeting bore down on Albert as he returned to his office. The agenda had been "Alignment of Leadership Thought Processes" – a seemingly abstract concept, but one that Albert recognized had profound implications. For Gorilla Inc. to progress cohesively, the need for leaders at all tiers to be on the same wavelength was paramount.

In this meeting, an insightful comment from a board member resonated with Albert, "We need to move beyond hierarchical leadership and adopt a blueprint of like-mindedness. Exceptional management is not about uniformity but about unity of purpose."

This sparked a profound realization in Albert. His role wasn't just to manage but to align his team's visions and ideas with the larger corporate narrative. The challenge was to craft a leadership model that resonated at every level of the managerial hierarchy.

Albert began by holding brainstorming sessions with his team, keenly listening to their insights, apprehensions, and aspirations. Instead of dictating directives, he posed open-ended questions, probing them to think critically about their roles in line with Gorilla Inc.'s objectives.

As these sessions evolved, Albert noticed a transformation. His team began to see beyond their immediate tasks. They started aligning their daily actions and decisions with broader company goals. The discussions also surfaced latent leadership potential within the team – individuals who, when given a chance, showcased their capacity to think strategically.

Emboldened by the success at his team level, Albert proposed an inter-departmental collaborative session. Leaders from various departments convened, shedding their designations at the door. This gathering was not about seniority but about synchronicity.

The sessions were revelatory. Teams that traditionally operated in silos discovered intersections in their objectives. They began crafting joint initiatives, pooling resources, and sharing best practices. Through open dialogue, leaders started identifying and rectifying misalignments in their strategies, ensuring that the entire organization moved in concert.

Albert's endeavor culminated in a detailed blueprint titled "Crafting Like-Minded Leadership." This document distilled the insights from the collaborative sessions, offering a roadmap for ensuring cohesive leadership across Gorilla Inc. It emphasized the importance of regular inter-departmental dialogues, the need for leaders at all levels to align their team's objectives with company goals, and the benefits of nurturing latent leadership potential within teams.

When Albert presented the blueprint to the board, it was met with unanimous approval. But for Albert, the real victory lay in the transformative journey – from isolated pockets of leadership to a harmonious symphony of like-minded leaders.

Reflection: Albert's exploration into crafting like-minded leadership serves as a testament to the power of collective thought. Leadership isn't about isolated decisions from the top but about crafting a shared vision that resonates through every layer of the organization. When leaders, irrespective of their rank, come together with a unity of purpose, the organization doesn't just function – it thrives.

Influence of Middle Management on Leadership Narratives

Middle management occupies a distinctive position in the corporate hierarchy. They are the bridge between top-level executives and frontline employees. Their role isn't just pivotal in translating strategy into execution but also in enhancing, modifying, and sometimes, even challenging the strategic narratives shaped by senior leadership. Given this critical role, the influence of middle management on rooting leadership narratives in strengths cannot be ignored.

Middle managers are often the first to recognize if a leadership narrative is inauthentic or inconsistent with a leader's actions. They ensure that the story shared by the leaders isn't just rhetoric but is supported by tangible actions. They can validate a leader's strengths and experiences, serving as a credibility checkpoint for the narrative.

While senior leadership might craft a strategic narrative, middle managers are the ones who translate this story into actionable steps for the teams they manage. They break down high-level strategy into tasks and projects, ensuring alignment with the overarching vision. Their intimate knowledge of day-to-day operations and challenges allows them to add depth and detail to the narrative, making it more relatable and tangible for frontline staff.

Middle managers interact directly with diverse groups within the organization. As a result, they have an innate understanding of what resonates with different demographics, including millennials. They can tailor the narrative, emphasizing elements that matter most to their audience, ensuring it remains relevant and compelling.

Middle managers provide a feedback loop to senior leadership. They offer insights on how well the narrative is being received, where there might be skepticism or confusion, and what elements are most inspiring. This feedback is crucial for leaders to refine their narrative continually.

While leadership may be responsible for setting the tone of stability, compassion, trust, and hope, middle managers are essential in ensuring these values are lived every day. Through their actions, decisions, and interactions, they reinforce (or challenge) the narrative set by leadership.

Often, middle managers serve as role models, embodying the leadership narrative in their actions. When they base their leadership style on their strengths and align their actions with the narrative, they serve as live examples, making the narrative more tangible and believable.

Middle management's influence on leadership narratives is profound. While top leadership might craft the story, it is the middle managers who bring it to life, refine it, and ensure it remains rooted in the leader's authentic strengths. Recognizing and harnessing this influence is crucial for organizations aiming to create a compelling and authentic leadership narrative that resonates throughout the organization.

CEO Perspective:

The Pivotal Role of Middle Management in Shaping Leadership Narratives

In my years serving as a CEO, I've come to realize that the backbone of any successful organization is not its cutting-edge technology or even its unique business models, but rather its people. And within that, middle management holds a particularly significant role. They are the often-underappreciated architects of the leadership narratives that guide our companies. This chapter aims to elucidate the multifaceted roles middle managers play in interpreting and implementing leadership visions, shaping company culture, and acting as a two-way communication channel between the top and bottom tiers of an organization.

The Interpreters of Strategy

Middle managers stand at the intersection between executive decision-making and operational execution. While executives lay out strategic directions, middle managers are the ones who interpret these directives into actionable plans for their teams. It's akin to translating a concept into a working language that everyone on the ground can understand and act upon. This interpretation isn't a mere replication; it requires keen insight into both the company's larger objectives and the unique dynamics and capabilities of their specific teams. Thus, middle managers play a critical role in adapting strategies to the real-world conditions and challenges their teams face.

Cultural Custodians

Company culture is not crafted by beautifully worded mission statements or declarations from the executive suite alone; it's shaped and lived in the corridors, meeting rooms, and even virtual spaces where teams actually work. Middle managers are the custodians of this living culture. They translate abstract values into the concrete behaviors that people adopt in their day-to-day tasks. They set the tone, modeling the sort of conduct that aligns with the company's stated values, thereby playing a crucial role in building an organizational culture that can sustain the business through its ups and downs.

A Two-Way Communication Channel

Middle managers are not just conduits for passing information downwards; they also serve as sensors, feeding information upwards to inform executive decision-making. They're uniquely positioned to understand the pulse of the organization—be it team morale, operational bottlenecks, or emerging opportunities. This feedback is invaluable for the C-suite, as it adds layers of granularity and nuance to the data we use to make decisions.

The Need for Investment in Middle Management

Given these crucial roles, it becomes evident that middle managers need to be armed with a certain skill set—ranging from strategic understanding to leadership acumen and effective communication abilities. Investment in developing these competencies is not a luxury; it's a necessity for organizational success. This is more than just sending them to week-long training programs; it's about fostering an ecosystem where they have access to continuous learning opportunities, mentorship, and practical experiences that enhance their abilities.

In my time as CEO, I've found that organizations that overlook the crucial role of middle management in shaping leadership narratives do so at their own peril. Middle managers have the potential to be your most effective leadership multiplier, carrying your strategic visions forward with nuance and adaptability. They can turn abstract strategy into meaningful work, and aspirational values into actual behaviors. The role they play in both interpreting leadership directives and feeding back operational insights is invaluable for business success.

To put it simply, if leadership narratives are the stories that guide and inspire our organizations, then middle managers are their most impactful authors and editors. Therefore, if we wish to see our companies not just survive but thrive in today's complex business landscape, then investing in the development of our middle managers is not merely beneficial—it's absolutely vital.

"Albert" Navigating the Middle: Albert's Influence on Leadership Narratives

The vast corridors of Gorilla Inc. were replete with tales of corporate giants, visionary leaders, and strategic masterminds. Yet, in the midst of this constellation, a star was steadily rising, redefining leadership paradigms. That star was Albert, a middle manager, who was reshaping the contours of leadership narratives from the heart of the organization.

Middle management, often likened to the "belly" of the corporate beast, is frequently overlooked in tales of transformative leadership. The spotlight predominantly shines on C-suite executives who chart out visionary strategies. However, as Albert's journey showcased, the true mettle of these strategies is tested, fine-tuned, and sometimes even reshaped in the crucible of middle management.

Albert had begun his tenure as a manager with the usual zeal of a newbie. However, he soon realized that his position, sandwiched between top-tier leadership and frontline teams, offered a unique vantage point. He was privy to the boardroom's lofty strategies and the ground-level challenges in actualizing them.

This dual perspective birthed in Albert a profound insight: middle managers weren't mere conduits for top-down directives but influencers who could reshape leadership narratives. Their proximity to both strategic decision-making and on-ground realities positioned them as the organization's real "pulse-readers."

Albert began leveraging this insight, gathering feedback from his team, understanding their challenges, and juxtaposing these against the company's strategic goals. Instead of merely cascading directives, he started crafting narratives, weaving the broader company vision with the specific needs, aspirations, and challenges of his team.

He also initiated dialogue with senior leadership, armed not with complaints but solutions. By doing so, Albert subtly but surely started influencing leadership strategies, bringing to the fore the on-ground realities and insights that only a middle manager could offer.

Word of Albert's innovative approach began to spread, challenging the traditionally held notions about middle management's role. His counterparts started adopting his methods, realizing that they too, could shape leadership narratives, ensuring they were more grounded, pragmatic, and holistic.

Albert's journey did more than just elevate his position within Gorilla Inc.; it shed light on the pivotal role of middle managers in crafting leadership stories. It underscored the fact that genuine leadership wasn't about hierarchical positions but the ability to influence, inspire, and instigate positive change from wherever one stood in the organizational chart.

Reflection: Albert's odyssey within Gorilla Inc. illuminates the often-underestimated power of middle management. It serves as a reminder that true leadership is decentralized, emanating from every corner of an organization. When middle managers rise to their potential, they don't just implement strategies; they influence, shape, and sometimes even redefine them, ensuring the organization's heartbeat remains robust and resonant.

Word from a CEO - The Ripple Effect of Management's Attitude

In the diverse tapestry of organizational life, the threads of management play a significant role in holding everything together. As the CEO, my perspective offers a unique vantage point from which I've observed the intricate patterns of our work culture. One observation that stands out starkly and requires our collective attention is a sentiment that's been voiced in hushed tones: "It feels like some of our managers just don't care as they should." Let's delve into the profound implications of this sentiment.

At its core, management is as much about human relationships as it is about strategies, budgets, and timelines. Employees naturally look up to managers. They seek not just operational guidance but also inspiration, motivation, and validation. A manager's perceived disengagement or lack of concern can send a deeply unsettling message to their team.

When managers appear aloof or distant, the repercussions are felt far and wide in their respective departments:

- Erosion of Trust and Morale: Employees, sensing a lack of appreciation or value, start to feel disenfranchised. This can erode the foundational trust and morale that bind teams together.
- Diminished Motivation: A manager's lack of enthusiasm or engagement can sap the energy from a team. Absent inspiration and direction, even the most dedicated employees might find their motivation waning.
- Talent Attrition: A pervasive feeling of being undervalued can prompt our best talents to look

elsewhere, leading to a talent drain. This not only incurs recruitment costs but also results in the loss of invaluable institutional knowledge.
- Impact on Production and Revenue: Over time, these factors coalesce to have a tangible impact on our deliverables and, ultimately, our revenue. A decline in team productivity can stall projects, compromise product quality, and challenge our financial health.

Understanding Managerial Detachment

Before jumping to conclusions or casting blame, it's crucial to empathize with and understand our managers. They, too, are navigating a myriad of challenges:

Overwhelming Workloads That Stretch Their Capacities

- A potential lack of training or resources to manage evolving challenges.
- External personal challenges that might spill into their work life.
- A sense of detachment from the broader company vision.

Grasping these underlying issues can pave the way for meaningful interventions.

Steering a Constructive Path Forward

Cultivating Effective Leadership Through Managerial Training

Training and nurturing managers is a foundational aspect of a thriving organization. The approach taken towards managers is often a reflection of the company's broader ethos and directly impacts the treatment of staff at all levels. It's a ripple effect – how managers are treated sets the tone for how they, in turn, treat their subordinates.

It's imperative to instill in managers a sense of value and self-worth. Recognize their contributions and affirm their roles as pivotal players in the company's success. Instead of reprimanding them when they don't meet expectations, it's beneficial to proactively provide them with the tools, training, and mentorship they need to excel. This relationship should be grounded in mutual respect, understanding, and continuous learning.

Additionally, fostering a culture of ongoing communication and feedback is crucial. Building strong relationships with managers based on trust and open dialogue allows for a more collaborative approach to problem-solving. Managers, when equipped with both, the soft and hard skills, through tailored training programs, are more likely to become effective leaders who can inspire, motivate, and guide their teams.

Furthermore, managers should be trained not just in the tasks specific to their roles but also in interpersonal skills, conflict resolution, and emotional intelligence. Their success isn't merely about completing tasks but about nurturing relationships, building teams, and creating an environment where everyone feels valued and empowered.

In essence, the relationship with managers should be rooted in nurturing their growth, emphasizing their intrinsic worth, and supporting their professional journey. When managers are well-supported and well-trained, they are better positioned to lead their teams with confidence, compassion, and competence.

Managers form the critical nexus between leadership and the broader workforce. Their attitude, engagement, and energy significantly influence team dynamics and, by extension, the entire organization's trajectory. By understanding and addressing the roots of managerial disengagement, we can foster a culture where managers lead with commitment, empathy, and passion.

Embracing Individuality in Management: A Call for Authentic Leadership

Management structures in any organization can sometimes resemble a chain, where each link, from the CEO down to entry-level employees, plays a pivotal role. However, it's essential to remember that every link, every individual, has its unique composition, strengths, and areas for growth.

Managers, like all employees, are individuals first. They come with a diverse array of experiences, insights, and qualities that make them who they are. It's unfair and unrealistic to expect a manager to be a carbon copy of their superior or to embody the exact characteristics of someone else in the organization. The superior is a superior, hopefully for a reason. They must accept and teach their staff, not show anger and demise.

Moreover, while work ethic and knowledge are fundamental, they are not the only metrics to gauge a manager's capability. After all, if they were solely judged by these criteria, they wouldn't occupy their current positions. Everyone has a unique value proposition that they bring to the table, and for managers, it's often a blend of technical know-how, leadership potential, and interpersonal skills.

Vice Presidents or senior leaders should guide and mentor rather than judge. Expectations should indeed be clear and high, but they must also be realistic. Every person, regardless of their position, has a learning curve, and it's the responsibility of senior leaders to ensure that middle managers are equipped with the right tools, knowledge, and support to meet those expectations.

Working through challenges should be a collaborative endeavor. When faced with dilemmas or obstacles, the focus should be on finding solutions together rather than placing blame. After all, a team's strength isn't just about the individual capabilities of its members but also about how they come together to complement each other.

Furthermore, clear communication is the bedrock of effective leadership. It's unreasonable to be frustrated with someone for not meeting an expectation if that expectation hasn't been clearly communicated. Training, regular feedback sessions, and open channels of communication ensure that everyone is aligned and working towards the same goals.

While the hierarchical nature of organizations is often necessary for functional and operational reasons, it's crucial to remember the human element. Every manager, every employee, is an individual, deserving of respect, understanding, and the right support to help them succeed. Embracing this ethos will not only lead to more harmonious workplaces but also drive innovation, productivity, and growth.

CEO Perspective:

Embracing Individuality in Management: A Call for Authentic Leadership

When I started my journey as a CEO, one of the first lessons I learned was that there is no one-size-fits-all model for effective leadership or management. While various schools of thought offer frameworks, principles, and best practices, the actual fabric of leadership is far more nuanced. Every manager, every team, and every business context is unique, and this chapter aims to delve into why and how embracing individuality in management is not just beneficial but necessary for authentic leadership.

The Fallacy of Formulaic Leadership

One of the pitfalls organizations frequently stumble into is adopting a formulaic approach to leadership. The thinking here is that if something has worked once, it should be replicable. But even the most successful case studies offer, at best, principles that must be adapted to your particular context. I've seen highly competent middle managers struggle when they attempt to apply the same strategies that worked for them in past roles or different organizational settings. The reality is that leadership is situational and requires a great deal of adaptability.

Authenticity as a Leadership Asset

People generally have a keen sense of detecting pretense. Authenticity in leadership is an asset that cultivates trust and fosters a more open, collaborative environment. Authentic leaders understand their strengths and weaknesses and are unafraid to show vulnerability. This doesn't mean revealing all your cards or getting too personal; rather, it's about being genuine in your interactions and consistent in your values and actions.

The Importance of Self-Awareness

Before a manager can lead authentically, they must first understand themselves. Self-awareness involves not just knowing your personality traits but also understanding how you react under stress, what motivates you, and how you impact others. This level of insight can be cultivated through introspection, feedback, and even formal assessments. And it's a continual journey, not a one-time event. As you grow and change, so too will the nuances of your leadership style.

Individuality in Team Dynamics

Understanding the individuality of your team members is equally important. The most effective managers I've seen are those who don't just manage teams but also manage individuals within those teams. They take time to understand each team member's skills, aspirations, and communication styles. This individualized approach allows managers to assign roles more effectively, resolve conflicts more amicably, and mentor in a more targeted way, ultimately creating a stronger, more cohesive team.

Encouraging Individuality Among Managers

For those of us in executive roles, it's essential to encourage a culture where middle managers can bring their authentic selves to work. This means not mandating a singular style of leadership but rather promoting a framework that allows for flexibility and personalization. Provide development programs that focus on cultivating a broad set of leadership capabilities and encourage managers to choose the approaches that align best with their authentic selves.

The business landscape is ever-evolving, influenced by technological advancements, market dynamics, and societal changes. Amidst all this, the principle of individuality in management stands as a constant. From my vantage point as a CEO, embracing individuality is less about defying convention and more about creating an authentic, adaptive leadership style that resonates with your unique personality and the specific needs of your team and organization.

To foster a culture of genuine, effective leadership, we must break free from the shackles of formulaic approaches. By investing in the self-awareness and development of our managers and promoting a culture that values authenticity, we're not just strengthening our middle management layer; we're fortifying the very foundations upon which our companies are built. And in an increasingly complex and competitive world, that is an investment well worth making.

Albert's Epiphany: The Mosaic of Individuality in Management

Gorilla Inc. had a tradition. Every quarter, department leaders would present their teams' successes and strategies to the rest of the company. This was an occasion Albert always looked forward to, providing insights into the various cogs that kept the corporate machine running.

However, over time, Albert noticed a pattern. Presentations, irrespective of the department, started to look and sound eerily similar. The same jargons, the same strategies, the same goals. It was as if a singular mold of management was being replicated across the board. The uniqueness, the distinct flavors of each team seemed to be dwindling.

It wasn't that the strategies presented were ineffective, but Albert couldn't shake off the feeling that something was missing. The absence of individuality, of a personal touch, seemed palpable. He wondered if, in the pursuit of a unified company culture, the essence of individual leadership was getting overshadowed.

Determined to delve deeper, Albert decided to have candid one-on-one chats with some of the department heads. He began with Diana, the head of Marketing, known for her creative campaigns. To Albert's surprise, Diana admitted, "I've been following the playbook, Albert. It seemed safer to adopt strategies that were tried and tested, rather than risk introducing my own ideas and facing potential failures."

Albert heard similar sentiments from other leaders. There seemed to be an unspoken fear of deviating from the norm, of showcasing one's unique leadership style.

Realizing the wealth of untapped potential, Albert initiated "The Authentic Leadership Retreat." A two-day offsite event, its primary goal was to encourage leaders to recognize, embrace, and celebrate their unique managerial styles.

The retreat had sessions on self-awareness, where leaders mapped out their strengths, weaknesses, and values. There were exercises on authenticity, teaching them to align their leadership with their personal values. One of the most impactful activities was the "Leadership Story Circle." Here, each leader narrated a personal story of a leadership challenge they faced and how they overcame it, not as a Gorilla Inc. manager but as themselves.

As the retreat concluded, there was a palpable shift. Leaders felt empowered to infuse their individuality into their managerial styles. The next quarter's presentations were a testament to this change. While the core values of Gorilla Inc. remained consistent, each presentation was imbued with the unique flair of the leader behind it. It was as if a monochrome tapestry had transformed into a vibrant mosaic overnight.

Reflection: Through Albert's intuitive observation and proactive initiative, Gorilla Inc. underwent a subtle yet profound transformation. It showcased that while a unified vision is essential, it's the unique colors of individual leadership that add richness to the corporate canvas. Authentic leadership doesn't dilute company culture; it enhances it. Albert's journey underscores the power of authenticity in leadership, proving that individuality is not a divergence but an asset.

Leading By Example: The Power of Action in Upper Management

In the dynamic and complex tapestry of organizational culture, one truth remains consistently clear: the behavior of upper management and business owners sets the tone for the entire organization. The ripple effect of their actions, decisions, and behavior cannot be understated. Employees look upwards for cues, guidance, and, most importantly, examples of how to navigate the daily challenges and triumphs of the business world. In essence, to influence and inspire staff truly, those at the top must lead by example.

The Shane Brodil Paradigm: The Thirst to Get Ahead

In the realm of managerial effectiveness, few figures stand out as starkly as Shane Brodil. He isn't just a manager; he's a dynamic force in the workplace, consistently outpacing his peers in both results and leadership ability. Shane's story offers invaluable lessons on how a thirst for self-improvement and a hands-on approach can revolutionize your management style and significantly impact your team.

An Unquenchable Thirst for Knowledge and Action

Shane Brodil doesn't merely rest on his laurels or settle for mediocre results. He has an insatiable hunger for knowledge, consistently challenging himself to learn new skills, concepts, and strategies. But what sets him apart is that he doesn't just learn; he applies what he's learned in real-world scenarios. This proactive application turns theoretical knowledge into practical wisdom, making him a well-rounded leader who knows the ropes and isn't afraid to navigate the ship through turbulent waters.

Shane's proactive, knowledge-based approach instills a high level of respect among his staff. They don't just see him as a boss but as a mentor, someone who doesn't just delegate but leads by example. His team knows that Shane won't ask them to do something he wouldn't do himself. And this isn't limited to intellectual tasks or strategic decisions; Shane is equally willing to "pick up the broom" and do the dirty work. This boots-on-the-ground attitude fosters a culture of collective responsibility, leaving no room for the sentiment of "that's not my job."

Every manager needs a role model, and Shane Brodil serves as an exemplary one. His example demonstrates that managerial effectiveness is not just about supervising a team but actively contributing to its skills, morale, and overall well-being. Managers who see their higher-ups, like Shane, involved in the grind feel more empowered to do the same. This creates a trickle-down effect of enthusiasm, work ethic, and commitment to the organization's goals.

The mentorship aspect is crucial too. A manager who has a role model has a clear path to follow, something that's particularly useful in times of uncertainty or change. Mentorship also promotes the sharing of critical soft skills that are often not part of formal training but are essential for managerial success. By having a mentor, managers gain a confidential space to discuss challenges, brainstorm solutions, and receive constructive criticism, enabling them to grow both professionally and personally.

The Shane Brodil paradigm isn't merely a methodology; it's a cultural shift. It implies a change in how we perceive the role of a manager, recognizing that leading by example and maintaining a relentless focus on self-improvement sets the stage for team excellence. Shane's approach suggests that the best managers don't just manage people; they inspire them. They don't just assign tasks; they roll up their sleeves and work alongside their team. They don't just meet goals; they exceed them through a blend of skill, tenacity, and an unwavering commitment to progress.

In a rapidly evolving business landscape, the Shane Brodil paradigm offers a timeless lesson: greatness in management stems from an unyielding commitment to growth—of oneself, one's team, and one's organization. So the next time you find yourself in a managerial dilemma, ask yourself, "What would Shane Brodil do?" Then, pick up that metaphorical (or literal) broom and get to work. Your team, and your future self, will thank you.

The Weight of Action

Words, mission statements, and values can articulate a company's ethos. Still, it's through tangible actions that these values are genuinely realized and internalized by the staff. The adage "actions speak louder than words" holds in business as it does in life. When a CEO demonstrates commitment by staying late to meet a deadline or when a manager rolls up their sleeves to help the team during crunch time, it sends a powerful message of solidarity and dedication.

The Multi-Dimensional Leadership of Robert Malmanger: From Calls to Coaching

In the current business landscape, where specialization is often the norm, Robert Malmanger stands out as a versatile leader. Not confined to the corner office, Robert is as likely to be found on a sales call as he is in a strategy meeting. His multifaceted approach to management serves as a model for those looking to make a real impact on their teams and organizations.

A Leader Who Wears Many Hats

Many managers delegate tasks and then remove themselves from the front lines of daily operations. Robert, however, subscribes to a different philosophy. He's not afraid to pick up the phone to make a sales call, troubleshoot a customer issue, or offer technical assistance. His hands-on approach extends to the more traditional aspects of management as well, such as strategic planning and team development. By being a jack-of-all-trades,

Robert showcases the importance of understanding and participating in multiple facets of the business.

Robert's willingness to engage in various roles does more than display his skills; it demolishes the hierarchical barriers that can impede teamwork and collaboration. When team members see their manager actively involved in different aspects of the work, it creates a culture of humility and shared responsibility. Robert's behavior sends a powerful message: every role matters, and everyone, regardless of rank, has something to contribute.

One of Robert's most commendable qualities is his commitment to staff development. He doesn't just perform tasks to get them done; he uses them as training opportunities for his team. Whether he's demonstrating how to close a sale or outlining the strategy behind a marketing campaign, Robert views each action as a teachable moment. This creates an environment where learning is integrated into daily work, accelerating the skill development of his team.

The Malmanger Model: An Integrated Approach to Leadership

What makes Robert's style of management particularly compelling is that it seamlessly blends hard skills, like sales techniques, with soft skills, such as effective communication and empathy. This well-rounded approach prepares his team for the complex, multi-disciplinary challenges they will face in the business world.

Moreover, Robert shows that good management isn't just about reaching targets; it's also about raising the bar for what a manager can and should be. A leader, in the Malmanger model, is not just an administrator but an active participant, a coach, and a perpetual student of the industry.

As the workforce evolves, managers would do well to adopt Robert's integrated style of leadership. By being deeply involved in both the granular and big-picture aspects of business, they can inspire their teams to new heights of achievement and job satisfaction. So, the next time you find yourself shying away from a task you could delegate, consider it an opportunity not only to contribute but to lead by example, the Robert Malmanger way.

The Visibility of Leadership

While the day-to-day grind can sometimes cloud the bigger picture, it's imperative for business leaders to maintain a visible presence among their teams. This doesn't mean micromanaging but rather showing genuine interest in the work being done and the people doing it. It can be as simple as walking the office floors, engaging in casual conversations, or regularly checking in on projects and offering help where needed. This visibility underscores a sense of unity and shared purpose.

Cultivating Trust Through Authenticity

Trust is the bedrock of any successful relationship, and in businesses, it's no different. Staff members can quickly discern between genuine actions and those done for optics. Authenticity in leadership means making decisions with integrity, acknowledging mistakes, and being transparent about the organization's challenges and successes. An authentic leader gains the trust and respect of their team, making them more likely to reciprocate those values in their work.

Empathy and Understanding

Understanding the challenges and aspirations of staff members is essential. By actively listening and empathizing, upper management can better align company goals with the individual goals of its employees. It fosters a sense of belonging and mutual respect, leading to increased motivation and commitment.

Investing in Growth

Leaders who actively invest in the professional and personal growth of their employees create a culture of continuous learning and development. It could be through training, workshops, or simply giving opportunities to take on more responsibilities. This not only boosts morale but also ensures the company evolves and stays competitive.

The influence of upper management and business owners extends far beyond strategic decisions and fiscal responsibilities. By actively embodying the values, work ethic, and commitment they hope to see in their staff, they set a standard that inspires and drives the entire organization. In an age where company culture plays an integral role in success, leading by example is not just a noble ideal but a strategic imperative.

The Indomitable Spirit of Sean Egiziano: A Lesson in Grit, Dedication, and Servant Leadership

In an age where work-life balance and the "four-hour workweek" capture the collective imagination, Sean Egiziano stands in sharp contrast. His work ethic echoes the old-school dedication that built empires, yet his approach is refreshingly modern and people-focused. Here's a man who doesn't just walk through fire; he does it while carrying his team on his shoulders.

The First to Arrive, the Last to Leave

One of the most striking aspects of Sean's leadership style is his work ethic. Arriving before dawn and leaving only when the sun has long set, Sean sets an example that goes beyond mere punctuality. His early arrival isn't about clocking in extra hours; it's about preparation, about setting the stage for the day's challenges. When he leaves long after others have clocked out, it's not just to catch up on work but to evaluate the day's outcomes and plan for the future.

An Insatiable Appetite for Challenge

While some might see additional responsibilities as a burden, Sean thrives on them. Challenges are not obstacles but opportunities in his eyes. Whether it's stepping into a role he's never tried before, taking on tasks outside his job description, or accepting criticism as a pathway to improvement, Sean's willingness to embrace difficulty is one of his most inspiring traits.

Perhaps one of Sean's most impressive balancing acts is his ability to maintain a hard line while exuding genuine care for his team. He can deliver tough feedback or make difficult decisions without alienating those around him. This duality is no small feat and speaks volumes about his emotional intelligence. He can demand excellence and hold people accountable while still fostering an environment where everyone feels valued.

Sean's dedication is not self-serving; it's rooted in a deep desire to see everyone around him succeed. In many ways, he embodies the essence of servant leadership. He's the first to volunteer for projects, not to showcase his skills, but to set a precedent of proactive involvement. He thrives on difficult tasks, not for the accolades, but because overcoming challenges can serve as a teaching moment for others.

The Egiziano Ethos: Building a Legacy of Resilience

Sean Egiziano's approach to leadership offers a robust model for aspiring managers and veterans alike. He shows us that dedication and hard work never go out of style but also emphasizes that a modern leader's strength comes from lifting others up, not pushing them down. He proves that taking on challenges head-on not only advances your career but can also inspire an entire organization.

So if you ever find yourself hesitating before a new challenge, or contemplating whether to take on more responsibility, think of Sean. Embrace the extra work, the steep learning curves, and even the criticism. For it's through facing these challenges that you build not just a career but a legacy. And in the process, you uplift those around you, crafting a narrative of collective triumph. This is the way of Sean Egiziano, a leader for the modern age with timeless values.

CEO Perspective:

Leading by Example: The Power of Action in Upper Management

> *"I will clean the restrooms, I will mop the floors, I will serve lunch...and I do daily!"*
>
> -Tobias

In my tenure as a CEO, I've always been struck by the old adage that actions speak louder than words. Nowhere is this truer than in the upper echelons of an organization. Whether we like it or not, every action we take—or don't take—sends ripples throughout the entire company. This chapter will explore why leading by example is not just a catchphrase but an operational imperative for upper management, with lasting consequences for middle managers and their teams.

The role of upper management, including the CEO, C-suite, and other top executives, goes beyond decision-making and strategy formulation. Every action, big or small, becomes a signal that staff throughout the organization will interpret—and these interpretations can either align with or distort the company's mission, values, and strategic objectives. Therefore, it's crucial to be keenly aware that your actions are under constant scrutiny and will often be magnified due to your position within the company.

Ethics and integrity are not just bullet points in a corporate brochure; they must be lived values originating at the very top. It's not sufficient to merely talk about ethical practices; upper management must walk the walk. Failure to do so will not only damage public and internal trust but will also tacitly give middle management and their teams permission to cut corners, setting a dangerous precedent throughout the company.

Leading by example offers a potent way to inspire middle managers. When they see upper management working diligently, showing up prepared, making informed decisions, and dealing respectfully with employees at all levels, it motivates them to mirror these qualities. Inspirational leadership thus trickles down the organizational hierarchy, motivating not just middle managers but also frontline employees.

In any organization, mistakes are bound to happen. How upper management handles these situations sets the standard for the entire company. Openly acknowledging errors, taking corrective action, and learning from missteps demonstrates a mature approach to accountability. It provides middle managers with a blueprint for handling their own and their team's errors, fostering a culture where accountability is viewed as a collective responsibility rather than a point of blame.

In today's fast-paced business environment, innovation is not a luxury; it's a necessity. Upper management can encourage a culture of innovation not just by funding R&D or adopting the latest technologies, but by actively participating in brainstorming sessions, encouraging cross-departmental collaborations, and being open to unconventional ideas. Such actions signal to middle managers that innovation is not just accepted but actively encouraged.

In the final analysis, leading by example is an unwritten contract between upper management and the rest of the organization. It says, "I won't ask anything of you that I'm not willing to do myself." This form of leadership provides a guiding star for middle managers, helping them navigate their own roles and inspiring them to set examples for their teams in turn.

As CEOs and top executives, our actions carry a weighted significance. Through conscious, consistent, and responsible behavior, we can set the tone for an organizational culture that amplifies our core values, encourages ethical conduct, and inspires every level of the company to strive for excellence. Leading by example is not merely a leadership style; it's a commitment to the sort of integrity, responsibility, and excellence that upholds the reputation and sustains the success of the entire organization.

A Mop, A Mission, and a Message: The Importance of Hands-On Leadership — A CEO's Perspective

There's a saying that you shouldn't ask someone to do something you wouldn't be willing to do yourself. While it may be an old adage, it's one that holds an important truth, especially in the realm of leadership. The symbolic act of a CEO willing to "mop the floors" or "clean the restrooms" isn't about showcasing a set of skills in janitorial services; it's about demonstrating a type of leadership grounded in humility, empathy, and a deep connection to all aspects of the business. Let's delve into why such gestures can be pivotal for both a CEO and the entire organization.

Being willing to engage in tasks that are generally considered "below your pay grade" sends a strong message of humility. It breaks down the often all-too-rigid hierarchical structures within a company, humanizing the CEO role. When employees see you're not above any task, they're more likely to respect you, not just for your title but for your character.

The willingness to roll up your sleeves and work alongside your team promotes a culture of shared responsibility. It sends the message that every task and every role is important for the success of the company. This can be a motivating factor for employees, encouraging them to take ownership and pride in whatever they do, irrespective of their role.

Walking a mile in someone else's shoes—or spending an hour on their job—can give you valuable insights into the challenges and difficulties they face. This sense of empathy makes you a more effective leader by enabling you to make decisions that are more informed and considerate of your team's everyday experiences.

Beyond the symbolic message, the practical experience of performing various jobs within your organization can provide you with critical operational insights. You'll gain a firsthand understanding of what works, what doesn't, and what could be improved, as well as the information you can use to make more informed strategic decisions.

By being willing to work across different departments and roles, you're also facilitating interdepartmental communication and cooperation. Silos can be detrimental to an organization's health, stifling innovation and cooperation. Your example can serve as a catalyst for increased collaboration and a more unified vision across the company.

The act itself becomes a story that is likely to be retold within the company, serving as an enduring lesson on the type of culture you wish to establish. It serves as a cultural touchstone that can be invoked in future discussions about company values, work ethics, and expectations.

The symbolic act of a CEO willing to engage in ground-level tasks is more than just a publicity stunt or a feel-good initiative. It's a leadership lesson in humility, empathy, shared responsibility, and unity. By setting such an example, you're not just telling your team what kind of culture you want to build; you're showing them. The ripple effects of this small act can extend far beyond the immediate moment, fostering a healthier, more engaged, and more cohesive workplace for years to come.

Albert's Legacy: Knowledge Sharing and the Ripple Effect of Leadership

It was a regular Wednesday morning, and Albert sat in his office, reflecting on the performance metrics for the past quarter.

While the figures were decent, Albert knew that 'decent' wasn't the benchmark Gorilla Inc. aimed for. The company was renowned for its cutting-edge innovations, and he felt that the management layer was not operating at its full potential.

As a seasoned manager, Albert had acquired a treasure trove of knowledge, strategies, and techniques that had served him well throughout his tenure. An idea sparked: what if he took on the role of a mentor, sharing his experiences and strategies with his team? Instead of holding onto his managerial secrets, he could empower his staff by offering them a deeper understanding of the nuances of effective leadership.

With this vision, Albert initiated the "Management Mastery" sessions. These were bi-weekly workshops where he would discuss various facets of management, ranging from problem-solving techniques to strategic planning. However, Albert ensured that these sessions weren't just lectures. They were interactive, peppered with real-life examples, challenges he faced, and the solutions he crafted.

To Albert's delight, the response was overwhelming. The staff, hungry for practical insights, began attending these sessions religiously. What stood out was how Albert didn't paint himself as an infallible leader. Instead, he candidly discussed failures, underscoring them as invaluable learning experiences. This approach demystified the process of decision-making, making it more approachable and replicable.

As weeks turned into months, a palpable shift occurred within the managerial ranks of Gorilla Inc. Managers began adopting the strategies discussed, tweaking them to suit their teams' unique needs. Decision-making became more streamlined, inter-departmental collaborations flourished, and a culture of continuous learning took root.

But the real magic occurred when these managers began mentoring their own teams. Using Albert's model, they began sharing their experiences and insights, creating a ripple effect of knowledge dissemination. It was as if Albert had ignited a flame, which was now spreading, illuminating every corner of Gorilla Inc.

The next quarterly review painted a vivid picture. Productivity metrics had soared, but more importantly, the engagement and morale of the teams were at an all-time high. Managers felt empowered, and their teams reaped the benefits of this newfound confidence.

Reflection: Albert's decision to share his managerial wisdom was more than just a training initiative. It was a testament to the power of transparency in leadership. By allowing his team a peek behind the curtain, he fostered trust, empowerment, and a culture of collective growth. The chapter reiterates a timeless truth: true leaders don't create followers; they create more leaders. Albert's legacy at Gorilla Inc. wasn't just about impressive performance metrics; it was about instilling a culture where knowledge became the bridge to excellence.

Final Chapter: In Reflection: The Tapestry of Effective Leadership

As we draw this exploration to a close, it's essential to pause and reflect upon the myriad facets of leadership and organizational success we've traversed. Leadership, as we've come to understand, is not a solitary act but a collective endeavor. It's about the subtle interplay between words and actions, the nuances of trust and authenticity, and the imperative of always leading by example.

When Leadership Fears Its Managers: The High Cost of Emotional Decisions

In an ideal organizational structure, managers report to leaders, and leaders guide managers. However, when leadership becomes afraid of its own management team, a paradox emerges. Instead of leadership acting as the pilot of the ship, it becomes hostage to its crew. The result? A myriad of problems that often culminate in significant financial losses.

The Root of the Fear

Leaders may fear confrontation, poor morale, or even the risk of losing skilled managers who are problematic in other ways. This fear often manifests as leniency towards managers who are not performing up to par. Unfortunately, avoiding confrontation doesn't solve the problem; it exacerbates it. Leaders who ignore underperforming managers due to emotional considerations are essentially setting the stage for organizational failure.

Ignoring the Red Flags

The reluctance to act can make leaders turn a blind eye to managers who consistently fail to inspire their teams, don't meet KPIs, or undermine company culture. Letting these issues slide not only demoralizes the workforce but also sets a dangerous precedent: it signals that mediocrity is acceptable. Over time, this attitude can erode the organization's financial stability.

When decisions are made based on emotional comfort rather than rational analysis, the organization suffers. For instance, neglecting to confront a manager who consistently fails to meet targets can lead to project delays, increased operational costs, and missed revenue goals. While it may feel easier to maintain the status quo, the financial ramifications can be crippling. Not to mention the loss of competitive advantage in an ever-demanding market.

At some point, the numbers will make it impossible to ignore the issue any longer. But by then, the cost of change can be significantly higher. You may be forced to lay off employees, scale back operations, or even face bankruptcy. The long-term effects of not addressing managerial problems can be devastating.

Leaders must overcome the emotional barriers that prevent them from holding managers accountable. This involves a mix of self-awareness, courage, and strategic planning. Regular performance reviews, audits, and employee feedback mechanisms can offer an unvarnished view of managerial effectiveness. Armed with this data, leaders can make informed decisions and, if necessary, plan for the replacement or retraining of underperforming managers.

The key is to establish an organizational culture where both leaders and managers are held to the same performance and ethical standards. This minimizes the room for emotional decisions that do not serve the company's best interests. Instituting a culture of accountability and performance can help maintain focus on the company's financial health and long-term sustainability.

Leadership cannot afford to be paralyzed by fear or emotional considerations when it comes to making tough managerial decisions. The stakes are too high. An organization can recover from financial losses, but recovering from a broken culture and tarnished reputation is far more challenging. Being forthright about problems and tackling them head-on is the only way to ensure that the organization remains viable and thrives in a competitive landscape.

In our journey, we've understood the profound weight of actions in the realm of leadership. Whether in the everyday tasks or strategic decisions, the choices made by those at the helm shape the ethos and trajectory of the entire organization. Actions do indeed speak louder than words, and they reverberate through the hallways of companies, setting precedents and defining cultures.

Visibility and presence have emerged as cornerstones. In a world increasingly dominated by digital interfaces, the human touch remains irreplaceable. The simple acts of being present, engaging with staff members, and genuinely understanding the ebb and flow of the organizational ecosystem create a sense of unity, belonging, and shared purpose.

Trust and authenticity, those seemingly elusive virtues, have been underscored as non-negotiable. In an age of information overload, discerning the genuine from the superficial becomes ever more crucial. Leaders who lead with authenticity, who aren't afraid to acknowledge their missteps, and who transparently communicate their vision sow the seeds of trust, fostering environments where innovation thrives, and employees feel valued.

Moreover, the emphasis on continuous growth and investment in development has shone brightly. The world, with its ever-evolving challenges and opportunities, demands adaptability and a commitment to learning. Organizations that prioritize the growth of their staff not only boost morale but also ensure they remain at the forefront of their industries.

To encapsulate, leadership, in all its complexity, is about weaving together these diverse threads into a cohesive tapestry. It's about recognizing that every action, every decision, and every word shapes the larger narrative of an organization. As leaders or aspiring leaders, the onus falls upon us to always be mindful of this responsibility, to lead with intention and purpose, and to create spaces where everyone, from the upper echelons of management to the newest recruits, feels empowered, valued, and inspired.

Thank you for embarking on this exploration of leadership with me. May the insights and reflections serve as a compass as you navigate the multifaceted world of organizational success.

The Foresight of William Cox: Mastering the Art of Pre-Emptive Leadership

In the world of management, it's not just about handling crises; it's about preventing them. And nobody embodies this principle better than William Cox. He's not just a problem-solver; he's a problem-anticipator. In a landscape filled with managers who are adept at "putting out fires," William is the one who smells the smoke long before others even strike a match. This chapter delves into the uncanny ability of William to call out red flags and preempt issues before they escalate, proving that the best kind of management is preventive.

William doesn't possess some mystical power, but his knack for sensing impending issues can almost make it seem that way. His intuition is honed by a combination of experience, keen observation, and an in-depth understanding of human behavior and organizational dynamics. These skills allow him to not just spot the red flags but to understand their potential implications deeply.

One of the key elements that contribute to William's success in anticipating problems is his commitment to open communication within his team. By fostering a culture where concerns can be raised without fear of retribution, he ensures that the early signs of trouble don't go unnoticed. However, the real magic lies in how he interprets these signals. Where others might see minor issues, William sees the first domino in a chain reaction that could lead to a bigger problem.

By calling out these red flags early on, William not only saves time and resources but also spares his team the stress and demoralization that come with dealing with crises. He understands that in the long term, prevention is less costly than cure—both financially and in terms of team morale.

Balancing Caution with Innovation

While his risk-averse approach might seem to stifle innovation or slow down progress, William has mastered the art of balancing caution with the need for forward momentum. His aim is not to prevent change but to manage it effectively. He encourages innovation but also insists on due diligence.

Trust and Empowerment

William's ability to anticipate problems has another less obvious but equally important benefit: it engenders trust. His team knows that if they follow his lead, they are less likely to encounter unmanageable problems. This trust forms the basis for a more empowered, cohesive, and efficient team.

THE COX METHODOLOGY: A BEACON FOR MODERN MANAGEMENT

In a fast-paced world where issues can spiral out of control in the blink of an eye, William Cox stands as a beacon for modern management practices. His proactive approach, founded on open communication, trust, and a deep understanding of the intricacies of organizational behavior, sets a new standard for effective leadership.

If you find yourself reacting more than planning, extinguishing fires more than building firewalls, then it's time to take a page out of William's book. Anticipate, communicate, and preempt. It's not just about averting crises; it's about creating an environment where they are far less likely to occur in the first place. And in doing so, you won't just be solving problems—you'll be creating a legacy of leadership.

Rebuilding Trust: Leadership's First Step Post-Crisis

Once the fear is addressed and the necessary changes are made, it's crucial for leadership to rebuild trust within the organization. This involves not just telling but showing all levels of the workforce that mediocrity will no longer be tolerated and excellence will be the new standard. Open and honest communication is key here: employees will appreciate transparency about past mistakes and the steps that are being taken to rectify them.

Metrics and KPIs: The Language of Accountability

Going forward, leadership should rely on quantifiable metrics and KPIs (Key Performance Indicators) to measure performance, not just for managers but also for themselves. This analytical approach removes emotion from the equation, making it easier to focus on what truly matters for the organization's success.

Aligning Team Goals with Organizational Objectives

One of the most effective ways to ensure that everyone is on the same page is by aligning individual and team goals with the broader organizational objectives. This creates a sense of collective responsibility that can help prevent the reemergence of fear-based decision-making. Managers, now held accountable, are more likely to engage in behaviors that contribute to organizational success rather than detract from it.

Proactive leadership goes beyond managing day-to-day operations and firefighting crises. It emphasizes anticipating future needs, problems, and opportunities to better prepare an organization for what lies ahead. This approach can transform companies from reactive entities that are always scrambling to deal with challenges as they arise into agile, resilient organizations that are well-prepared to adapt to new situations. Here are some key aspects of proactive leadership:

Proactive leaders have a vision for the future and are always working toward it. They consider the long-term implications of their actions and decisions rather than focusing solely on short-term gains. This strategic perspective enables them to align organizational goals and resources effectively.

Instead of just reacting to problems as they occur, proactive leaders try to anticipate potential issues and put measures in place to mitigate these risks. This could range from diversifying revenue streams to guard against market fluctuations to implementing rigorous quality checks to prevent product failures.

Proactive leaders understand the importance of building a strong team around them. They recruit wisely, train diligently, and delegate effectively. By empowering team members to take on responsibilities and make decisions, leaders can focus on strategic planning and other high-level tasks, confident that daily operations are in capable hands.

Open channels of communication are vital for proactive leadership. Leaders not only need to communicate their vision and strategies effectively, but they also need to listen. Feedback from team members can provide invaluable insights into potential problems or opportunities that may not yet be on the leader's radar. The business landscape is continuously evolving, and proactive leaders know that they must evolve with it. This means staying updated on industry trends, technological advances, and best practices, but it also means fostering a culture of learning and adaptability within the organization.

While planning is a cornerstone of proactive leadership, so is the ability to adapt those plans when necessary. Whether due to unforeseen challenges or new opportunities, being too rigid can be as problematic as having no plan at all. Being proactive isn't just about anticipating business needs; it's also about understanding and managing emotional dynamics among team members. Emotional intelligence helps leaders gauge the mood within their teams, tackle interpersonal issues before they escalate, and maintain a positive work environment.

Proactive leaders use key performance indicators (KPIs) and other metrics to monitor both short-term and long-term performance. This data-driven approach allows them to spot trends, make informed decisions, and adjust strategies as needed.

Proactive leadership is about more than just taking initiative. It involves a multi-faceted approach that combines strategic planning, risk management, effective communication, and a commitment to continuous growth and improvement. By adopting these practices, leaders can position their organizations for long-term success, building resilience and agility into the very fabric of their corporate culture.

Fostering a Growth Mindset

In the new culture, adopting a growth mindset—where challenges are seen as opportunities for improvement rather than threats—can have a transformative effect. This shifts the focus from blame and fear to learning and development, creating a more adaptive and resilient organization.

Every Monday, I host a company-wide meeting focused on growth and mindset, assembling our team of 150 individuals to start the week on the right foot. These sessions serve as a rallying point, setting the tone for the week and providing a space to align our collective energies toward our objectives. We discuss key performance indicators for upcoming projects, and I often share motivational insights to foster a positive mindset. The aim is to not only update everyone on our business trajectory but also to cultivate an atmosphere of shared purpose and enthusiasm. These meetings are a cornerstone in our efforts to foster growth and production across the board, ensuring that each team member feels engaged, informed, and empowered to contribute to our company's success.

Retraining and Reskilling: Investments for the Future

Sometimes, the issue isn't necessarily with the people but with outdated skills or approaches. In such cases, instead of letting go of otherwise valuable managers, consider retraining or reskilling programs. This not only improves performance but also signals to the workforce that the organization is committed to their professional growth. It's essential to install regular checks and balances to ensure that the organization does not slip back into old, destructive habits. These could include regular anonymous surveys, periodic external audits, or even establishing an internal committee responsible for overseeing management performance.

Leading with Courage and Integrity

The cost of leadership fearing its managers is high—both in terms of finances and organizational well-being. To foster a successful and sustainable company, leaders must have the courage and integrity to make difficult decisions, even when those decisions are emotionally uncomfortable. With the right strategies and a steadfast commitment to excellence, leaders can navigate through turbulent waters, turning challenges into stepping stones for future success.

Investing in Emotional Intelligence: The Subtle Art of Leadership

As leaders take a courageous stance, investing in emotional intelligence becomes a necessity rather than a luxury. It's not just about understanding numbers and setting targets; it's also about connecting with employees at an emotional level to inspire and motivate them. Leaders need to empathize with their managers, understanding their fears and aspirations while also holding them accountable for their responsibilities.

The Symbiotic Relationship Between Upper and Middle Management

Leadership and management aren't isolated tiers but part of an interconnected ecosystem within the organization. For a company to truly recover from the financial downfall resulting from fear-based decisions and lax accountability, upper management must work symbiotically with middle management. This involves not just top-down but also bottom-up communication, where insights and feedback from middle managers are valued and acted upon.

Navigating the Complex Landscape of Change Management

Change is difficult but often necessary, especially when the status quo is causing the organization to hemorrhage money. Leadership needs to be skilled in change management, ready to make adjustments while also handling the inevitable resistance that comes with altering long-standing processes and expectations. This involves strategic planning, ongoing communication, and the allocation of sufficient resources to implement change effectively.

The Role of Vision in Restoring Financial Health

After any major shake-up, it's important for leadership to articulate a clear and compelling vision for the future. This serves two purposes. Firstly, it sets a direction for the entire company, something to aim for beyond simply 'recovering from a crisis.' Secondly, a strong vision acts as a rallying point for employees, boosting morale and providing a sense of purpose that can be particularly motivating during challenging times.

Navigating through a financial crisis requires a shared vision and collective action, something I emphasize when collaborating with my management team. I regularly convene focused discussions to strategize about restoring financial health, ensuring that each manager is aligned with our overarching goals. Thomas and I take this a step further by encouraging all staff members to view the crisis not just as a setback, but as an opportunity for innovation and growth. We implore everyone to make the most of the situation by identifying efficiencies, exploring new revenue streams, and being agile in their roles. By being transparent about our financial standing and proactive in our strategy, we create an environment where staff feel empowered to contribute positively, turning losses into learning experiences that shape our future success.

Building a Culture of Ownership and Initiative

In the long run, for the financials to truly turn around, a culture of ownership and initiative needs to be fostered at all levels. Managers who feel ownership of their roles and outcomes are far more likely to be proactive, to seek solutions, and to engage their teams effectively. This sense of ownership has a cascading effect, trickling down to even the newest team members, thereby increasing overall productivity and, consequently, financial health.

The Dawn of a Resilient Organization

Leadership that allows fear to dictate its relationship with management can plunge an organization into a financial crisis. However, crises can be valuable crucibles for change. By facing the hard facts, holding everyone—including themselves—accountable, and taking the necessary steps to instill a culture of excellence, resilience, and shared vision, leadership can navigate the organization out of choppy waters into a more prosperous and stable future. This is a journey that requires courage, vision, and, most importantly, action. It's time to steer the ship with a renewed sense of purpose.

The CEO and CFO Perspective: Synergizing for Organizational Resilience

Aligning Visions and Strategies

The CEO, as the ultimate leader and visionary of the organization, is chiefly responsible for setting the direction of the company. Meanwhile, the CFO brings a focus on financial health and sustainability, ensuring that the company's resources are allocated effectively. When both roles are perfectly aligned, it creates a potent synergy that can drive a business out of crisis and into a realm of sustainable growth.

The CEO's Role: Emotional Intelligence Meets Visionary Leadership

As the CEO, your responsibility extends beyond merely setting targets and expecting your managers to meet them. The essence of leadership lies in how you navigate relationships, foster a healthy culture, and cultivate an ecosystem of trust and performance. You set the vision, but it's equally crucial to involve your team—especially the CFO—in creating strategies to achieve that vision.

The CFO's Role: Realistic Guardrails for Grand Visions

The CFO's role in this process is critical. While the CEO will have a grand vision for the future, the CFO provides the fiscal responsibility required to make that vision achievable. This involves budgetary planning, risk assessment, and capital allocation, ensuring that the company's financial resources are optimally utilized to reach its objectives. The CFO also brings key insights about financial constraints or opportunities that might alter or sharpen the company's direction.

A common language between the CEO and CFO is essential for fostering cohesion and accountability in the organization. While it's the CEO's role to encourage and inspire the managers, the CFO can offer important data that may be crucial for effective decision-making. Managers should be held accountable through performance metrics that reflect both the CEO's vision and the CFO's strategic financial planning.

Operationalizing Vision Through Financial Strategy

For an organization to bounce back financially, it's not enough to simply cut costs; growth must be a core focus. The CFO, with their finger on the pulse of the company's economic health, can help operationalize the CEO's vision by setting achievable financial targets and KPIs. This quantitative expression of the vision provides a roadmap that managers at all levels can follow.

Navigating Change Together

Change is not just the domain of the CEO but a joint venture that requires the expertise and insights from the CFO as well. Financial data can offer invaluable feedback on the success of newly implemented strategies. With these insights, the CEO can fine-tune the vision, if necessary, and refocus the organization's energy where it counts the most.

A siloed approach to leadership and financial management is a surefire recipe for stagnation, especially in times of crisis. CEOs and CFOs who work in tandem, aligning vision with financial prudence, create an agile, responsive, and ultimately more resilient organization. The bond between them should be unbreakable, built on open communication, mutual respect, and a shared commitment to leading the company to new heights of success. This is the leadership formula that every struggling organization needs to master in order to turn the ship around and sail toward a brighter future.

Transparency and Clarity: Ensuring Managers are Aligned with the Company's Direction

The Necessity of Transparency

Both the CEO and CFO must champion transparency within the organization, not just between themselves. Transparency serves multiple purposes: it builds trust, improves decision-making, and creates a sense of shared purpose. For these reasons, it's crucial that the strategic directions decided upon by the CEO and CFO are openly communicated to middle and lower management.

Building a Culture of Trust

Trust is the bedrock of any organization. If managers don't trust the executive team, they won't be invested in executing the vision with enthusiasm or diligence. Transparency is how trust is earned. By openly discussing the rationale behind various decisions and strategies, managers are more likely to buy into them. This ensures that managers don't just execute orders; they internalize them, becoming champions of the vision themselves.

In our organization, building a culture of trust is paramount, and it begins with treating every team member as an equal. I firmly believe that the most fruitful work environments are those where every voice is heard and valued, irrespective of title or tenure. To establish and nurture this sense of trust, I maintain an open-door policy, inviting everyone to share their thoughts, concerns, and suggestions freely. Furthermore, decisions are often made collaboratively, emphasizing that each person's input is not only welcomed but is vital to our collective success. By fostering this egalitarian atmosphere, we create a climate where trust is not merely a buzzword but the foundational element that shapes our team dynamics and propels us toward achieving our shared goals.

Improving Decision Quality

Transparency helps improve the quality of managerial decisions. When the CEO and CFO provide full information about the company's strategic goals and financial status, managers can better align their teams and resources to those objectives. This eliminates wasted effort and helps concentrate energy where it will be most impactful.

A Shared Vision

One of the greatest risks an organization can face is misalignment. When managers are not fully apprised of the organization's objectives and the financial constraints or opportunities that might exist, they may inadvertently steer their teams in directions that don't serve the organization's long-term goals. Open communication ensures that everyone from top to bottom is pulling in the same direction, sharing the same vision and understanding of what success looks like.

I make it a priority to regularly share my visions for our company with the management team, ensuring that we are all aligned in our strategic focus and operational execution. Utilizing dedicated planning sessions, quarterly updates, and ongoing dialogues, we delve into both our immediate goals and Big Hairy Audacious Goals (BHAGs) to make certain everyone is operating from the same playbook. By doing so, we create a unified sense of direction and ambition that permeates throughout the team. The collaborative setting allows for a two-way exchange, enabling managers to provide valuable feedback and insights that refine our objectives. This practice of shared vision and aligned goals serves as the backbone of our organizational strategy, driving us toward collective success.

Navigating Change and Uncertainty

Markets and circumstances change, often unpredictably. It's important that changes in direction or strategy are quickly communicated to management layers to ensure rapid and effective adaptation. The CEO and CFO must be united in presenting these changes and in providing the "why" behind the change so that managers can quickly align their teams and adapt. With clear communication and transparency, accountability naturally follows. Managers, fully aware of the strategy and expectations, are better positioned to set targets for their teams that align with the company's goals. This also allows upper management to hold them accountable in a fair and transparent way.

Transparency isn't just a buzzword; it's a fundamental aspect of effective leadership. CEOs and CFOs who prioritize open communication with their management layers empower them to act as force multipliers, dramatically amplifying the effectiveness of strategic initiatives. The more aligned everyone in the organization is, the more agile and responsive the entire ship becomes, capable of navigating through even the roughest of economic seas.

The Value of Belonging: Making Managers Feel Part of a Greater Mission

Emotional Investment: Beyond Monetary Compensation

We often talk about the hard metrics of business—revenue, growth percentages, and market share, among others. However, the soft metrics like morale, engagement, and a sense of belonging are equally essential. Managers are more than mechanical entities deployed to fulfill KPIs; they're emotional beings who will perform better when they feel a sense of attachment to the company's goals and culture.

The Role of Storytelling

One potent tool at the disposal of the CEO and CFO is storytelling. Sharing the story of the organization, how it came to be, its ups and downs, and its mission for the future can help to instill a sense of belonging among managers. When people understand the narrative they are a part of, they are more likely to invest emotionally in their roles. They don't just see a job; they see a story that they are helping to write.

Inclusion in Decision-Making Processes

While it may not be feasible or practical to include managers in every executive decision, finding opportunities for their voices to be heard can go a long way in making them feel like part of the bigger picture. This can be as simple as having regular forums where managers can express their ideas or as significant as involving them in strategy brainstorming sessions.

Inclusion is an affirmation of value, and it communicates trust in their judgment.

Transparency doesn't have to be a grand gesture; it can be as straightforward as periodic updates on the company's performance and upcoming plans. An open-door policy also helps to make managers feel that they are part of something larger. Knowing that they can discuss issues or ideas directly with higher-ups fosters a culture of mutual respect and open dialogue.

People want to feel seen and appreciated. Celebrating the victories, whether big or small, creates a sense of shared accomplishment. It's not just the company that succeeds, but every individual within it. Recognition for a job well done makes managers and their teams feel like vital parts of the organization, increasing their emotional investment in the company's success.

In some organizations, offering stock options or other forms of financial stakeholding can effectively make managers feel part of the enterprise. This aligns their financial success with the company's performance, which can be a powerful motivator.

When a manager feels like they belong, that they are part of something significant, this attitude often trickles down to their team. The entire team is more likely to be engaged, motivated, and productive, amplifying the effects of a positive culture throughout the organization.

For a company to reach its full potential, everyone needs to be pulling in the same direction. Creating a sense of belonging among managers is crucial for this. A manager who is emotionally invested in the company will go the extra mile, inspire their team, and contribute meaningfully to the company's culture and bottom line. CEOs and CFOs need to realize that the sense of belonging doesn't just happen; it needs to be actively fostered through consistent actions and clear communication. When you build a team where everyone feels like they belong, you build a team that will stand by you, no matter what challenges lie ahead.

The Downstream Impact: How Managers' Sense of Belonging Influences Their Teams

In an organization, managers act as the critical bridge between executive leadership and the frontline workforce. The attitudes, beliefs, and motivations of managers are magnified as they cascade down to the employees they supervise. Here's how a manager's sense of belonging and emotional investment can profoundly influence the team beneath them.

An Environment of Trust and Openness

When managers feel that they belong and are part of something meaningful, they are more likely to create an open and trusting environment within their teams. Employees feel more comfortable sharing their ideas, challenges, and even dissenting opinions, knowing they will be heard and respected. This kind of open communication is crucial for innovation and problem-solving.

Enhanced Employee Engagement

Managers who are emotionally invested in the organization tend to have contagious enthusiasm. Their outlook impacts how their team members view their work and the company. As managers speak positively about the company and its objectives, team members are more likely to become engaged and committed to their tasks and goals.

When managers feel a real connection to the company's mission, their leadership style tends to be more authentic. They are not just enforcing rules or pushing towards KPIs; they are guiding their teams in a shared mission. This form of leadership is more relatable and inspiring for team members, fostering a collective drive towards success.

Managers who feel like they are part of something significant are often more collaborative. They understand that collective success is personal success, encouraging them to break down silos and work cross-functionally. This collaborative spirit usually extends to their team, creating a more unified, less compartmentalized organization.

Empowerment and Delegation

Managers who feel trusted and valued by upper management are more likely to extend that trust to their team members. This leads to increased delegation and empowerment. Employees, sensing this trust, are more likely to take the initiative and ownership of their tasks, thus improving productivity and job satisfaction.

Employees are keenly attuned to their work environment, and a positive, inclusive atmosphere can be a powerful motivator for staff retention. When they see their managers genuinely invested in the company, it sends a strong message about the company's stability and desirability as a long-term place to work.

Beyond just the professional aspects, a sense of belonging contributes to the holistic well-being of employees. When the manager sets an example of work-life balance, continuous learning, and emotional intelligence, employees are encouraged to incorporate these elements into their own lives, resulting in a healthier, more balanced workforce.

When managers feel like they're part of something bigger, it creates a virtuous cycle that benefits everyone. The positive influence flows downstream, permeating various aspects of the workplace—from job satisfaction and team cohesion to innovation and overall productivity. For CEOs and CFOs committed to a thriving organization, investing in the emotional well-being of managers isn't just a nice-to-have; it's a strategic imperative. By making managers feel like they belong, you're not just improving their lives; you're enhancing the overall health of the entire organization.

THE TURNAROUND: LEADING THROUGH CRISIS IN THE COVID ERA

It was mid-2020, the world was gripped by the COVID-19 pandemic, and like many other businesses, we had to adapt rapidly. We shifted to remote work, hoping that our operations would continue with minimal disruption. But despite our best attempts to maintain normalcy, the reality was harsher than we anticipated.

Sales reps were calling out, productivity was dipping, and the energy and cohesion we had fostered in the office seemed to dissipate into the digital ether. Our once-thriving team was stagnating, and I knew that we had to do something to revitalize our spirit and performance.

After months of struggling, we made the tough call to bring the team back to the office, albeit in a staggered, socially-distanced manner, and following all public health guidelines. It wasn't an easy decision, and there was pushback from various quarters. However, we recognized the essential ingredient missing in our remote work model was the face-to-face interaction, that ineffable spark that drives collective productivity and keeps morale high.

We didn't just want people back in the office; we wanted them to feel like they were part of something bigger than themselves, especially in these trying times. To make the transition easier and motivate the team, we initiated some new policies:

1. Flexibility in Scheduling: Understanding that the pandemic had reshuffled personal responsibilities, we offered flexible working hours.

2. Health and Safety Measures: Sanitization stations, regular office cleanings, and mandatory masks were non-negotiables.

3. Open Communication Channels": We held bi-weekly town halls to discuss our vision for the future, share key performance metrics, and address any concerns openly.

4. Crisis Bonuses: To appreciate the extra effort put in during these times, we introduced a "crisis bonus," which was highly appreciated and boosted morale.

Slowly but steadily, we saw a transformation. The sales reps were energized, our team was brainstorming innovative solutions to navigate through the crisis, and there was a palpable sense of collective purpose. We were not just surviving; we were thriving amidst adversity.

This period taught us the irreplaceable value of in-person interactions, the resilience of our team, and the importance of proactive leadership. Had we not acted when we did and how we did, things might have turned out differently. It was a risk, but it was a calculated one, and it paid off.

Today, we're stronger than ever, not despite the pandemic but because of how we navigated through it. The experience proved that leadership is not just about sailing smoothly during calm waters but effectively steering the ship through the tempest, with everyone on board, towards a brighter dawn.

"Albert Closing in Reflection: The Tapestry of Effective Leadership"

The sun was setting, casting a golden hue across the Gorilla Inc. campus. Albert sat in his office, the same room where countless decisions had been made, strategies devised, and dreams envisioned. Amid the silence, he took a moment to reflect on his journey.

He remembered the early days, fraught with challenges and uncharted territories. There had been times when the sheer weight of responsibility had seemed overwhelming. Yet, as he delved deeper into the intricacies of leadership, Albert had come to realize that the heart of effective leadership lay not in power but in the delicate balance of trust, authenticity, and shared purpose.

Through his experiences, Albert had witnessed the ripple effect of his actions, both large and small. He saw how a single decision, taken with consideration and care, could set into motion a chain of events that impacted the entire organization. He understood that leadership was not just about directives from the top but about creating an environment where every member felt a sense of ownership and pride in their contributions.

In his interactions with employees across all levels, Albert learned the value of presence. The digital age, with its plethora of tools and platforms, could never replace the depth of human connection. Those casual chats by the coffee machine, the brainstorming sessions on a whiteboard, or the simple act of listening had cemented bonds, fostered trust, and allowed for genuine collaboration.

Albert had also come to treasure authenticity as a cardinal virtue. He recalled instances where admitting a mistake or being transparent about a challenge had led to innovative solutions simply because everyone felt they were on the same team, working towards a shared goal. The culture at Gorilla Inc. thrived not because of perfection but because of the authenticity and vulnerability that permeated its walls.

He thought about the many training sessions, workshops, and mentorship programs that had been initiated. Investing in the continuous growth and development of the team had reaped rich dividends. It had not only enhanced skills but also reinforced the message that every individual at Gorilla Inc. was valued and integral to its success.

As Albert gazed out of his window, he realized that leadership was indeed a tapestry intricately woven with threads of vision, empathy, dedication, and resilience. Each strand, no matter how thin, contributed to the grand design. Leadership was not about one person but about the collective, the shared journey towards a vision.

Closing his diary, filled with reflections, insights, and dreams, Albert felt a deep sense of gratitude. He had not just been a part of Gorilla Inc.'s journey but had played a role in crafting its legacy. A legacy where leadership wasn't just a title but a promise – a promise of trust, growth, and shared success.

And as he left his office, turning off the lights and stepping into the twilight, Albert left behind not just a blueprint for effective leadership but also a testament to the infinite possibilities that arise when one leads with heart, vision, and purpose.

FINAL WORDS: THE CHAIN REACTION OF PURPOSEFUL LEADERSHIP

In the complex machinery of an organization, managers act as pivotal gears connecting the vision of upper management with the hands-on execution of frontline employees. Their sense of belonging and emotional investment doesn't just stay with them; it cascades throughout their teams, affecting everything from trust and communication to collaboration and innovation.

When managers operate in an environment where they feel valued and part of something larger than themselves, the impact is multifaceted. It fosters an open atmosphere, spurs employee engagement, authenticates leadership styles, and stimulates collaboration across the board. Furthermore, it positively influences staff retention and overall well-being, creating a robust and resilient workforce ready to face challenges head-on.

This isn't merely a "feel-good" approach to management; it's a strategic imperative. For CEOs and CFOs, the equation is clear: emotionally invested managers lead to committed, productive teams, and that directly contributes to the organization's success. Therefore, it is critical to ensure managers not only know the company's direction but also feel intrinsically linked to its journey.

In essence, a manager's emotional and professional investment in the company acts as a catalyst, setting off a chain reaction of positivity and performance. This results in a corporate culture where everyone—from the top-level executives to the newest hires—feels engaged, motivated, and aligned with the company's goals. The ultimate beneficiary of this virtuous cycle is the organization itself, poised for sustainable growth and long-term success.

Solving Managerial Effectiveness: A Blueprint for Success

Even with the best intentions, managing effectiveness isn't an automatic outcome of well-articulated visions or grand strategies. It requires a deliberate approach, measurable metrics, and the commitment to continuously invest in both managerial and team development. Here are some pragmatic solutions:

Data-Driven Performance Metrics

Relying solely on anecdotal evidence to gauge managerial effectiveness is a recipe for subjectivity and potential bias. Establishing quantifiable key performance indicators (KPIs) enables organizations to measure managerial efficacy accurately. These KPIs can range from employee turnover rates under a particular manager to project delivery timelines and even customer satisfaction scores, if applicable.

The culture of feedback shouldn't be a one-way street where managers review employees without being reviewed themselves. 360-degree feedback systems, where superiors, peers, and subordinates can all offer insights, provide a holistic view of managerial performance. This should be a regular, perhaps quarterly, exercise rather than an annual event.

It's essential to remember that management techniques are not one-size-fits-all. Training programs should be adaptive, taking into account not only the company's immediate objectives but also broader industry trends, generational shifts in the workforce, and even global influences such as remote working dynamics. Managerial effectiveness isn't solely about delivering projects on time or meeting financial targets. It's also about navigating complex human emotions and facilitating a work environment where people feel valued and heard. Emotional intelligence workshops can equip managers with the skills to foster such environments.

It's vital to incentivize managers to keep learning and improving. This could be through bonuses tied to performance improvements, educational stipends for further study, or fast-tracking high performers for leadership roles within the organization.

Accountability should be designed into the organizational structure. If a manager is consistently failing to meet KPIs or is a constant subject of negative feedback, there should be a clear process for addressing these issues, ranging from additional training to, if necessary, considering a role change.

By combining these elements, CEOs, Owners, COO's, and executives (you) can develop a comprehensive strategy to improve managerial effectiveness across the board. When managers are competent, accountable, and emotionally invested, the ripple effect on their teams is profoundly positive, reinforcing a cycle of continuous improvement and long-term organizational success.

In closing, the role of effective management can never be overstated in shaping the culture, performance, and long-term success of an organization. As the business landscape undergoes rapid changes from technological advancements to demographic shifts, the task of ensuring managerial effectiveness grows both more complex and more urgent. This book has laid out the challenges, opportunities, and concrete strategies CEOs, CFOs, and other organizational leaders can employ to cultivate a robust managerial ecosystem. It is our collective responsibility to strive for not just good but great management, building resilient teams that can adapt and thrive in a perpetually evolving work environment. Remember, the true measure of effective leadership isn't just in quarterly reports but in the growth and well-being of the individuals who make those numbers a reality. Here's to your journey in elevating managerial effectiveness to new heights and securing a prosperous future for your organization.

Made in the USA
Columbia, SC
22 June 2024

00aa826a-d7fb-4531-91a5-8ba8c67e4be0R01